Investing for lazy investors

Tony Pow

Why you invest

You will need to learn about investing sooner or later in your life. You also need to take some calculated risks.

Compare the returns of the following assets: cash, CDs, treasury bills, bonds, real estate and stocks. We start with the risk-free investments and end with the riskiest. It turns out that the average returns are in the opposite order. Cash and CDs are not risk-free as inflation eats our profits. For example, the real return is negative for the 2% return in a CD and a 3% inflation rate. In addition you have to pay taxes for the 'returns'. <u>Our capitalist system punishes us for not taking risk</u>.

There are two kinds of risk: blind risk and calculated risk. If you buy a stock due to a recommendation from a commentator on TV or a tip, most likely you are taking a blind risk. It would be the same in buying a house without thoroughly evaluating the house and its neighborhood. When you buy stocks with a proven strategy (i.e. when/what stocks to buy and when/what stocks to sell), you are taking a calculated risk. In the long run, stocks with calculated and educated risks are profitable.

Be a turtle investor by investing in value stocks and holding for longer time periods (a year or more). "Buy and Monitor" is a better approach than "Buy and Hold" as some could lose all the value such as in the failure of Enron.

For experienced investors, shorting, short-term trading and covered calls would make you good profits. Simple market timing would reduce your losses during market down turns. If you buy a market ETF and use my simple market timing, you should have beaten the market by a wide margin from 2000 to 2019.

With so many fraudulent and poor managed hedge funds (but many exceptions), do not trust anyone with your investing. Do not buy investing instruments that are highly marketed such as annuity and term insurance.

If you are a handy man and do not mind to satisfy the constant requests of your tenants, buy real estate in growing areas that could be very profitable in the long run.

Take advantage of the tax laws such as investing in a 401K especially the part that is matched by your company and/or a Roth IRA.

Why you need this book

All my techniques in making big money are described in this book. My children are not interested in investing, and hence there is nothing for me to hold back.

- As of 2021, I made more than **4 times profit** using sector rotation with an investment more than my yearly salary then.

- I recommended 20 stocks in an article Amazing Return in Seeking Alpha. If you bought them on the published date, you would have beaten the S&P500 index by over 100% in a year without considering dividends.

- I achieved 80% return in my largest taxable account in 2009. It could be the best time to buy stocks and I call it Early Recovery.

- I made 50% in a month in 2019 using Year-End technique.

- My incredible returns in the last 3 books of my "Best stocks to buy series" beat S&P500 by wide margins.

#Filler: Miss Mia

In my first job and just after the Vietnam War, everyone (yes, guys and ladies) tried to date my beautiful officemate Mia except me. If we married, then her name would be Mia Pow ('missing-in-action' and 'prisoner-of-war'). She would be very popular or very unpopular without showing her beautiful face. In any case, when she becomes a mother, she will be Mamma Mia.

Table of Contents

- Why you invest ... 2
- Why you need this book ... 3
- Introduction ... 8
  - Disclaimer ... 10
- Book 1: For the laziest investors ... 12
  - 1 Investing for 'lazy' folks ... 12
- Book 2: Riskier but more profitable investing ... 14
  - 1 Investing psychology 101 ... 15
  - 2 What to do with the list ... 16
  - 3 Year-end strategies ... 19
  - 4 My philosophy ... 24
  - 5 Newsletters and subscriptions ... 25
  - 6 Advantages of a retail investor ... 30
  - 7 Hedge fund 101 ... 33
- Book 3: Simplest market timing ... 37
  - 1 Simplest market timing ... 37
  - 2 The power of market timing ... 39
  - 3 Bubbles ... 42
  - 4 Actions for different stages of a market cycle ... 44
  - 5 Market timing by calendar ... 51
  - 6 Summary of investment calendar ... 55
- Book 4: Evaluate ETFs ... 57
  - 1 Quick analysis of ETFs ... 57
  - 2 An example ... 60
  - 3 ETFs / Mutual Funds ... 61
- Book 5: Trading Stocks ... 67
  - 1 Chronology of a trade ... 67
  - 2 Order prices ... 69
  - 3 Stop loss & flash crash ... 74
  - 4 Tax avoidance ... 77

5	Brokers	81
6	Money Market, CDs & Bonds	84
7	Covered calls	86

Book 6: Finding Stocks 89

1	Where the web sites are	89
2	*Finviz.com screener*	91
	A screener example	93
	Other sources	93
	Common parameters	95
3	Sectors to be cautious with	99
4	Fidelity	102
5	Performance of my screens	104

Book 7: Evaluating Stocks 107

1	Amazing returns	108
2	A scoring system	114
3	Simplest way to evaluate stocks	119

Section I: Fundamental metrics 123

4	Mysteries of P/E	123
5	*Fundamental metrics*	130
6	Finviz's parameters	140
	Your broker's website	147
	Other sources	147
	Gurus	148
	Quick and dirty	148
	5-minute stock evaluation	148

Section II: Beyond fundamentals 150

7	Intangibles	150
8	Qualitative analysis	154
9	Avoid bankrupting companies	158

Book 8: Strategies 160

1	Super long-term investing	160
2	How to hedge inflation	161
3	Making 20% return year after year	162
4	Insider Trading	163
5	Dividend Investing	165
6	Rotate four ETFs	168
7	How to find the current best-performing sectors	170
	Fidelity	170
8	SMA, MACD and Volume	170
9	Selling a winner	176

*** Bonus: Experiences 178

Section 1: Performance form "Best Stocks" series 179

1	Past Performances	179

Section 2: My experiences 187

1	Beginners' major mistakes	187
2	Super long-term investing	189
3	Vaccines and the investor	190
4	Lessons from my trading in 2019-2020	191
5	Lessons from selling GME	193
6	Disasters in 2020 and 2021?	195
7	How to prepare for disasters	197
8	Airlines	198
9	Value or Momentum?	200
10	When to close the shorts	201
11	Miscellaneous	203

Section 3: Gurus' experiences 204

1	Pointers from short-term gurus	204
2	Tips from Peter Lynch	205
3	Charles Munger: 12 common mistakes	207
4	Making 20% return year after year	208
5	From a guru (technical analysis)	209

6	Predictions for 2021	210
7	Disrupting innovation	212

Epilogue 213
    My parting gifts to you 214
Appendix 1 – All my books 214
    Best stocks to buy for 2022 (avail. after Dec. 15, 21) 215
Appendix 2 – Complete the Art of Investing 216
    Sector Rotation: 21 Strategies 220
Appendix 3 - Our window to the investing world 221
Appendix 4 - ETFs / Mutual Funds 222

Introduction

This book consists of 9 books (same as super sections). You should find at least one useful pointer from every page of this book compared to one or two pointers in most investing books.

This book represents decades of my investing experiences, extensive simulations and summaries of hundreds of books and YouTube videos I have read on investing.

It should make you a better investor from advanced beginners to fund managers alike. With proven, step-by-step techniques to time the market, find and evaluate stocks, it is closer to the Holy Grail of investing. The proven adaptive philosophy is using what has worked recently in fundamental metrics and stock searches.

My article "Amazing Returns" for Seeking Alpha, a popular site for investors, could provide the best performance from the published date to one year later recommending 10 or more stocks. So far, there has been no challenge to my claim. All the concepts and techniques behind this article were presented in this book in an easy way to read. This is the simplified and concise version of my book "Complete the art of investing" and it is targeted for beginners.

Your time is important. I have the briefest investing article in two pages (6*9). It is followed by "Riskier but more profitable" investing strategies. The next two books included describes simple market timing and evaluating ETFs.

"Trading Stocks" and "Advice" are described next.

The next three books are for future uses with advanced techniques on "Finding Stocks", "Evaluating Stocks" and "Strategies".

How to use this book
Most graphs and tables are in landscape orientation (recommended for small screens) for both paperback and e-readers. Some graphs may not be displayed adequately on a small screen of an e-reader. Use PC to read the graphs on the larger screen. For better orientation, just flip your e-reader device 90 degrees if it is available. Most e-readers let you select a table or a graph to display it to fit the screen.

The **font size** (Ctrl Minus for browser implementation of e-readers) should be adjustable.

There are clickable links to web articles. Most of them are from my own web sites and public web sites such as Wikipedia. Some public links may not be available in the future as they are not under my control and my book may change. For security, get the information such as "RSI(14)" directly from the source; the primary ones are Wikipedia, Investopedia, YouTube and Fidelity.

These links extend the usefulness of this book by making available specific topics that may not be interesting to every reader. It also provides articles (most are not written by me) for more in-depth analysis. Instead of typing the links to your browser, you can access the following web site to access most of the links easier
http://tonyp4idea.blogspot.com/2021/05/web-links-for-printed-copy-of-my-book.html

Fidelity provides video clips to explain some of the basic terms. Fidelity does not require a balance to open an account; I have no affiliation with them except I retired from Fidelity. Take advantage of their extensive research and info. YouTube offers similar video lessons. This book provides many of the links for the paperback readers. In any case, get the same information or extra information by entering a search in Wikipedia and/or Investopedia (http://www.investopedia.com/) such as "Dogs of the Dow".

'Afterthoughts' includes my additional comments and ideas of minor importance. There are fillers with tips, refreshing pictures (taken by me) and jokes (most original) to fill up some empty space of the printed book. Fillers, links and afterthoughts should not disrupt the flow of reading this book. So far, no one has asked me to take them out yet; many readers enjoy them and many treat them as breaks of reading this book.

For convenience, this book uses SPY, an Exchange Traded Fund (ETF) simulating the S&P 500, as the benchmark for the market. Annualized returns (Return * 365 / (Days between)) are used where appropriate for a more meaningful comparison. To illustrate, I had a 10% return in 6 months, a 10% in a year and a 10% in 2 years. It is more meaningful to use annualized returns of 20%, 10% and 5% respectively for the 6-month return, I use one-year return and the 2-year return in this example. Usually I do not include the dividend, so you can add an estimated 1.5% to the annualized return for SPY. In addition, compound interest is not used for easier calculation, so the actual return could be even better.

Since most of the stock recommendations are probably obsolete by the time you read about them, use them as examples and do not trade the mentioned stocks without consulting your financial advisor first. For simplicity, I treat ETN the same as ETF.

About the author
I graduated from Cal. State University at San Jose in Industrial Engineering and the University of Massachusetts in Amherst with a MS in Industrial Engineering. I have retired from a job in IT. I have been an investor for over 30 years and have written over 30 books on investing. Here is the link to some of the articles I have written.

Dedication
To all retail investors and future retail investors including my grandchildren.

Acknowledgement
Thanks to Seeking Alpha, Wikipedia and Investopedia for the many helpful links to enrich this book. Fidelity.com, Yahoo!Finance and Finviz.com for the tools and charts used in this book.

Important notices
© 2021-2022 Tony Pow

Version	
Initial	08/21
V1.1	11/21

No part of this book can be reproduced in any form without the written approval of the author. My email address is pow_tony@yahoo.com and my blog is https://tonyp4idea.blogspot.com.

Book store managers can order the printed books from Creatspace.com. https://tonyp4idea.blogspot.com/2020/12/book-managers.html

Disclaimer
Do not gamble with money that you cannot afford to lose. Past performance is a guideline and is not necessarily indicative of future results. All information is believed to be accurate, but there it is not a guarantee. All the strategies including charts to detect market plunges described have no guarantee that they will make money and they may lose money. Do not trade without doing due diligence and be warned that most data may be obsolete. All my articles and the associated data

are for informational and illustration purposes only. I'm not a professional investment counselor, a tax professional or any other field. Seek one before you make any investment decisions. Remember to consult with a registered financial adviser before making any investment decisions. The above mentioned also applies for all other advice such as on accounting, taxes, health and any topic mentioned in this book. Tax laws change all the time, so talk to your tax advisors before taking any action. Most of the time, I use annualized for a better comparison; 5% in a month is more than 4% in a year for example. For simplicity, most of my returns do not include commissions, exchange fees, order spread and dividends. It is the same for all the links contained in this book. Some articles may offend some one or some organization unintentionally. If I did, I'm sorry about that. I am politically and religiously neutral. I have provided my best efforts to ensure the accuracy of my articles. Data also from different sources was believed to be accurate. However, there is no guarantee that they are accurate and suitable for the current market conditions and /or your individual situations. The values of some parameters such as RSI(14) are arbitrarily set by me. My publisher and I are not liable for any damages in using this book or its contents.

Book 1: For the laziest investors

This is the shortest article (two 6*9 pages), but it Is highly effective.

1 Investing for 'lazy' folks

You have better things to do than investing or you do not have the time, the desire to learn and/or expertise in investing. You should be better off to buy ETFs.

I recommend the following 4 ETFs. If you have $100,000 to invest, buy $25,000 for each recommended ETF. Consult your financial advisor before taking any action. The recommended ETFs should have a large market cap (the ETFs themselves and not the stocks they hold) and have a high volume.

Most returns started on July 1 and ended on July 1 the following year; this article is written on July 20, 2021. All are annualized returns for easy comparison. Fees, commissions and dividends have not been included; you can add the dividend yield and prorate it for YTD return.

Symbol	Name	YTD[1] Return	1 Year[2]	5 Years[3]	Bear[4]
IWF	Russel 1000G	30%	34%	40%	-33%
QQQ	QQQ	30%	46%	42%	-31%
VTI	Vang. Viper Tot	34%	22%	42%	-35%
VUG	Vang. Growth	37%	33%	41%	-32%
Avg.		31%	34%	41%	-33%
SPY[5]		34%	21%	39%	-35%
Beat[6]		-9%	60%	6%	7%

[1] The start date is 1/4/2021 and the end date is 7/1/2021.
[2] The start date is 7/1/2020 and the end date is 7/1/2021.
[3] The start date is 7/1/2016 and the end date is 7/1/2021.
[4] The start date is 1/2/2008 and the end date is 4/1/2009. My estimates.
[5] SPY is the ETF for the S&P 500 index. It is used as a yardstick.
[6] = (Avg. − SPY) / SPY. Again it does not include fees, commissions and dividends.

Comments:

- The YTD is the only period that this portfolio does not beat SPY (the market to many). It could mean the market could be changing the favorite from growth stocks to value stocks. However, 31% return is far above the average of the market.
- The one-year return beats the market by 60%.
- The 5-year return beats SPY only by 6%, but the return of 41% is nothing to sneeze at.
- All except Vanguard's Viper Total are ETFs for growth stocks. Hence, I expected it would not beat the market, but it still did by 7%.
- You can time the market using the techniques described in this book as often as you can. When the indicator tells you to exit, you can sell these ETFs and reenter the market when it recovers. Riskier investors can buy contra ETFs such as PSQ and SH instead of holding cash when the market is down.
- At least once in a year review the selection. Use ETFdb.com for information. If you do not have time, it is fine skipping the review. When you switch ETFs, taxes should be considered.
- Most ETFs replace some stocks periodically to ensure better appreciation potential.

Book 2: Riskier but more profitable investing

You can subscribe an investment letter and follow the trades, or buy an mutual fund that perform well recently. However, it is risky as there are too many followers if they are successful.

You can buy my book in the "Best stocks" series. I should have one in July 15 and one in Dec., 15 every year. I do not have too many followers even the performances of the last books as of 7/2021 have been phenomenal. Past performances do not guarantee future performances. In any case, consult your financial advisor before committing any money.

Filler: Happy Mother's Day Poem

The following is my translation from poet Yu's work in Chinese. I changed some words as some could not be translated effectively. I added the title "Two Cries".

-------- Two Cries -----------

I cried at two unforgettable times in my life.

The first time when I came to this world.
The second time when you left this world.

The first time I did not know but from your mouth.
The second time you did not know but from my heart.

Between these two crises, we had endless laughs.
For the last 30 years, we had joyful laughs that had been repeated, repeated...

You treasured every laugh.
I cherish every laugh for the rest of my life.

1 Investing psychology 101

- Be emotionally detached. Do not gamble the money you cannot afford to lose especially for retirees. Use stops and trailing stops to protect your portfolio. My friend's friend died due to too much worries when the market was down. The market finally recovered but he did not.

- Learn from the history of your trades but never look back emotionally.

- Do not be jealous. Before 2000, a lot of value investors shorted the tech stocks. Many were jealous of the young fund managers making over 50% in a year on tech stocks. Hence, they followed them and lost big when the tech stocks collapsed. History repeated itself in trading bitcoins.

- Do not follow gurus blindly. Many gurus made big, but lost it all. Follow the gurus that have good track records from both the bull and bear markets.

- Do not invest in something you do not understand. I do not invest in bitcoins.

- It may not be profitable to use the same playbook on today's market as the market changes all the time.

  As of this writing in August, 2020, the poor economy does not affect the market a bit. It is due to excessive printing of money. Most likely the bad effects will come, but no one identifies when it will happen. I believe the market cannot sustain making high heights after the election. We're also running out of cash to further participate in this over-valued market. Stick with what you believe in the market; I bet that it works in the long run.

- The successful traders' winning trades were much larger than their losing trades. Even with a low winning percentage such as winning 30% of trades, many still come out ahead. You can be an investor (long term) and a trader (short term) at the same time.

- Do not take profits too early but use trailing stops.
- A related YouTube link.
https://www.youtube.com/watch?v=MGglyvc8d58

2 What to do with the list

Know yourself and the market

Are you a growth investor, dividend investor or value investor? You can be all. Today the market is risky, so most of the stocks in the list are value stocks. Last year was good for growth stocks. If the market is plunging, sell all stocks as evidenced by "Simplest Market Timing". When the market returns, reenter the market. At that time, reevaluate the stocks before you buy.

Simplest way to evaluate stocks

Here is a step-by-step instructions based on my current findings stocks for this list in the last chapter. All the information is available free from websites and most are up-to-date. However, sometimes I suspect the data are not correct.

All books including this one are not updated. Successful subscription services on stock selection are very expensive. Cheap subscription services must have a huge circulation that would deteriorate performance. Insiders of some subscription services buy the stocks before they publicize the stocks in their subscriptions. Do not depend on stock recommendations in public sites. It could be "pump-and-dump" especially on small stocks. If it is so promising, why the author gives them free?

Do your homework for better performance. Investing in stocks is a guess work. The better the education / work, the better the potential appreciation in theory; it is true in the long run from my personal experiences.

1. Fidelity.com (no charge to open an account). From Fidelity.com, select Research and then Stocks. To illustrate, enter the stock symbol such as ORCL. The Equity Summary Score (used to be the Analyst Score) should be 7 or higher. ignore this rating for year-end trades and short-term trades.

   From the same screen, the P/E (PE) should be positive and lower than the average P/E (PE5) of the last 5 years. As in the last chapter, I find out how much cheaper it is by the following formula. It is a buy at 10% or higher discount. The following is my example of ORCL on that particular date.

Cheaper % = -(PE − PE5) / PE5
= -(18,23 − 25.96) / 25.96 = 26%

There is a lot of other information and a chart that gives you everything you want to know about the stock. Refer to Technical Analysis chapter for the chart and technical events.

Many articles are written for Oracle. Finviz.com and Seeking Alpha are other sources. Do not trust the articles 100% as the analysts may have to meet their employers first. However, they estimate earnings better.

2. Yahoo!Finance. Bring up Yahoo!Finance and enter ORCL. Select Statistics. "EV/EBITDA" is better than P/E as it considers debts and cash. I call EBITDA/EV true EY (earnings yield).

3. Finviz.com. There is a lot of duplicate information from other sites. However, Insider Transactions is quite useful and it should be higher than -10%. Scroll to the end to check whether the Insider Transactions makes sense, and I found several times it did not.

Some value investors do not buy stocks when SMA200 is negative. I usually skip stocks with "Debt / Eq." higher than 3. It also depends on the sector. For example, utilities need to borrow a lot.

"Forward P/E" is based on the estimates from analysts. I value it as a better indicator than "P/E". "EPS Q/Q" and "Sales Q/Q" (quarter to quarter) are good momentum indicators together with SMA20 and SMA50.

"Forward P/E" in the ORCL example is 14 and great for a tech company (passing grade is 25 and 20 for most other sectors). "Debt/Eq" is high at 2.37 and "P/B" is very high at 7.84 but it may not include all the intelligent properties. Fidelity gives it a good score but Finviz's re the "Recom" is rated average. The colors red / green in Finviz.com show below / above recommendation.

Know the company. Finviz.com shows the following:

"Oracle Corporation develops, manufactures, markets, sells, hosts, and supports application, platform, and infrastructure solutions for information technology (IT) environments worldwide. The company provides services in three primary layers of the cloud: Software as a Service, Platform as a Service, and Infrastructure as a Service.

It offers human capital and talent management, enterprise resource planning, customer experience and relationship management, procurement, supply chain management, project portfolio management, business analytics and enterprise performance management, and industry-specific application software… Oracle Corporation was founded in 1977 and is headquartered in Redwood City, California."

4. Read articles on the stock listed by Fidelity.com, Finviz.com and/or Seeking Alpha (with less free articles today) depending on your time available for researching stocks. This is the qualitative analysis / intangible analysis of your research.

#Filler: The endless wars

It causes us countless lives and countless resources in our endless wars from Vietnam to today's Afghan. We never learned from the French on Vietnam and the Russians on Afghan. When we do not learn from history, most likely we will repeat history.

How many countries sent their National Guard to the front line?

3 Year-end strategies

There may be a list of stocks for year-end losers in the next book published in 12/15/2022 (not a promise).

I have two: 1. Buy the current year winners (YEW) and 2. Buy the current year losers (YEL).

The first strategy is riding the institutional investors' window dressing to include the winners in their funds to make them look better. It did not work well in 2018, so I skip it in 2019.

The second strategy takes advantage of selling losers for tax purposes. We need to find value stocks, but not stocks that are heading into bankruptcy. I had amazing returns in 2018 and will continue this strategy in 2019.

The following describes how to create your own testing if you have a historical database. It would be a frame for testing other strategies.

- Define the starting date. For the first strategy, I would use 9/1, 10/1 and 11/1 for two sets of test data. For the second strategy, I would use 12/1 and 12/15. Check to see which starting date is better for the specific strategy.
- Define the durations, the number of months before you sell the purchased stocks. I use 1 months, 2 months, 3 months and 6 months for my designated durations.
- Define the number of tests. I would start from the year 2000, one or two years older if your historical database allows for that. Actually I started in the last 3 years or so to save time. However, do not use dates older than 1995 as the market was quite different then.
- Compare your results to SPY (or the S&P 500 index).
- Ignore dividends for simplicity.
- Use annualized rates for a better comparison.
- If the date has no data such as during holidays and weekends, use the date after it for consistency.
- Take out stocks that would not be the stocks you usually would buy, such as penny stocks (that likely boost the performance due to survivorship bias), small foreign companies and/or stocks giving huge dividends or giving a return of capital.

- Use different metrics to sort, such as Expected Earning Yield (E/P) or a composite grade. Use the top 5 (or 2) stocks to calculate performances.
- Include the maximum drawdown (the maximum loss from recent height) from many selected time frames (i.e. durations described). My maximum loss is -52% from 12/1/2007 to one year later in my Year-End Loss strategy, but followed by a 256% gain in the next year.
- Negative percent numbers could give you wrong calculations when comparing to an index. Check them out manually if your formula has not taken care of the negative numbers.
- A year-end winner strategy should include large companies (traded by fund managers) and stocks that have increased in values year-to-date.
- From my limited testing, my small-cap stocks are better than other stocks and they have to be profitable.
- Here are my best results for the two strategies. Again, my results will not be the same as yours due to different selection criteria. Past performance may not have anything to do with future performances.

The year-end loser strategy in 2015 does not work that well as I screened many stocks that were scored very low. I found out many screened stocks were from foreign countries. Many emerging countries have had problems and I do not trust most of their financial info. Besides that, many were energy companies which I already had too many of.

Many have Expected Earning Yields over 35%. However, most have very high debts such as Debt/Equity is over 1 (i.e. 100%). If I bought them, I would unload them within 3 months fearing a market crash in 2016 [Update. As of 2019, we do not have one]. Historically, it is profitable, but I may skip most YEL stocks this year as most were deserved losers. The lesson is: Adjust to the current market conditions.

Strategy	Starting Date	Duration	Avg. Annual. %	Max. Drawn Down
YE Winners	10/1	4 months	40%	-36%
YE Losers	12/1	6 months	42%	-28%

My experience. When trying to make good money, you need to find a strategy that matches the current market. Here are my recent strategies I actually tried with real money in 2018.

* You usually see window dressing from institutional investors from Nov. 1 to Dec. 1 (some use dates earlier than Nov. 1). Buy the current winners and sell the current losers of stocks with a large market cap.

The market was risky so I did not buy winners but shorted some losers.

* Buy year-end losers from Nov. 1 to Dec. 31 (some use dates earlier than Nov.1). The companies have to be profitable (>15%), big losers (most having over 50% yearly loss) and small companies (preferred).

Incorporate the strategy with today's volatile market (i.e. buy when they plunge and sell when they rise). You need to determine what is a "plunge" and a "rise". For me, it is short-term and the percent is 5% from a recent high or low.

There is a selling part of these strategies I have not included here. Most of my strategies are based on exhaustive tests from historical data with a lot of work.

Every market is different. We need to make a lot of adjustments. From my experiences, the best research may not make you money all the time. In the long run, the more educated you become, the better chance for you to make money.

Year-End 2018
This was one of my best monthly returns. The average purchase date is 12/27/2018 and the current prices were based on 1/28/2019. The return is 53% or 648% annualized. Most likely the performance will not be repeated. However, it serves as a procedure for coming years.

I change the quantity Q to 1. Several stocks have been purchased more than once. I sold 3 stocks already indicated by the Status = 'Sold'. 'JT' is my own taxable account described here.

Account	Screen	Year-end loser	Start	12/21/19	End	1/8/2019	Today	1/28/19		
Stock	Q	Buy	Sell	Buy $	Sell $	Buy Date	Sell Date	# Days	Profit $	Profit %	Ann %	Status

Stock	Q	Buy	Sell	Buy $	Sell $	Buy Date	Sell Date	# Days	Profit $	Profit %	Ann %	Status
401KC												
CHK	1	2.13	2.99	2	3	01/03/19	01/18/19	15	1	40%	982%	Sold
MNK	1	16.41	21.45	16	21	01/03/19	01/25/19	22	5	31%	510%	Sold
MNK	1	16.43	21.45	16	21	01/03/19	01/25/19	22	5	31%	507%	Sold
NNBR	1	5.68	8.58	6	9	12/26/18	01/28/19	33	3	51%	565%	
NNBR	1	5.72	8.58	6	9	12/26/18	01/28/19	33	3	66%	727%	
ESTE	1	4.35	6.45	4	6	12/26/18	01/18/19	23	2	48%	766%	Sold
JT												
LCI	1	4.61	8.29	5	8	12/21/18	01/28/19	38	4	80%	767%	
MDR	1	8.01	9.13	8	9	01/08/19	01/28/19	20	1	14%	255%	
YRCW	1	3.29	5.78	3	6	12/21/18	01/28/19	38	2	76%	727%	
YRCW	1	3.26	5.78	3	6	12/21/18	01/28/19	38	3	77%	742%	
401K												
ASRT	1	3.56	4.18	4	4	12/26/18	01/28/19	33	1	17%	193%	
UTCC	1	7.13	11.00	7	11	12/26/18	01/28/19	33	4	54%	600%	
YRCW	1	2.92	5.78	3	6	12/26/18	01/28/19	33	3	98%	1083%	
Tot/avg				84	119	12/27/18		29	36	53%	648%	

I sold my YRCW (not shown above) on the earnings date that can be found from Finviz.com. When the earnings are positive, it will be sold for my asking price plus a little more but less than the surge. If it is negative, it will not be sold. I recommend to canceling any trade order before the earnings date.

As of 09/07/2019, LCI is up by 185% and YRCW is down by 27% (I sold one position in my retirement account for about 100% gain).

Year-End 2019

As expected I did not gain 50% in a month but I made a decent profit. The "Gain %" are good based on data on 1/18/2020 and no dividends and fees are considered. HOFT has been bought two times. If the "Sell Date" is blank, it means I still own the stock on 1/18/2020. This portfolio is heavily weighted in energy stocks.

My own trades that have an average of 4.7% for the month:

Stocks (11)	Buy Date	Sell Date	Gain %
HOFT	12/04/19	01/14/20	4%
HOFT	12/06/19	01/15/20	11%
METC	12/03/19	01/02/20	14%
REI	12/09/19	01/03/20	35%
EGY	12/10/19		25%
SND	12/10/19		0%

SBOW	12/17/19		-19%
SD	12/17/19		-17%
URBN	12/20/19		3%
GT	12/11/19		-8%
CAL	12/11/19		-4%

The performance of the stocks listed in my book "Best Stocks for Year End 2019" is 4.6%. The 2018 result of 53% in a month is not sustainable, but beating the SPY (without considering fees and dividends) by 19% is nothing to sneeze at.

If I only include the 4 stocks from the recommended 9 that have Earnings Yield (forward earnings) more than 20%, I would have a return of 10%. I went back to 2018 year end. If I selected the top 4 highest Earnings Yield, I would get about 40% (vs. about 30% for all 8 stocks). I will select stocks according to this finding in the next book titled "Best Stocks to Buy in 2021" shortly available after Dec. 15, 2020. It is not a promise for the book. There are some stocks not included in my actual trades.

Stocks (9)	Gain %
CAL	-4%
EGY	25%
HOFT	0%
METC	17%
REI	10%
SCOR	6%
SND	-12%
URBN	-2%
ZAGG	2%
Avg.	4.6%
SPY	3.87%
Beat SPY	19.1%

How long should we hold these screened stocks? Except those in my taxable account, I sold all of them in the first two months. The following is the annualized returns for holding 1 month, 2 months, 3 months and 5 months (as of 6/22/2019). From my previous testing, I should have held the stocks for 6 months. However, I have made my objective already and I want to take advantage of this volatile market. I could not find UTCC in my historical database. I sold it with an annualized return of 572%. It could be acquired or merged.

The following tries to determine what would be the best holding period for these stocks. For simplicity, I used 12/27/2018 as the purchase date for all stocks. I consider one position for each stock even though I bought it several times. Hence, my three purchases of YRCW is considered as one purchase here. Again, I do not include dividends, the bid spread and commissions.

	1 Month	2 Months	3 Months	5 Months
Ann. Return	497%	366%	178%	17%
SPY	72%	74%	52%	31%

From the above, I did well in selling most of them. If I held all of them for 5 months, they would not beat the SPY, which is used as the market for comparison purpose.

4   My philosophy

When you pay $25 or less for this book, do not expect it always makes you money, as no one can guarantee that. It is a good step to reevaluate the stocks again, as the market could have been changed. If the market is risky, do not buy any stocks at all and close some risky positions.

The performances of the recommended stocks in my last three books have been phenomenal. I do not expect it will continue forever. Here is my philosophy in screening and evaluating stocks.

- Most of my recommended stocks are value stocks and they should be held long term (one year for me) except the short-term stocks and stocks for year-end strategy. Hence, they should do better than the market when it is plunging.
- If the market is moving high due to the irrational surge of the momentum stocks such as in 2020, my selections may not do as well as the market, but they would move up with the tide. Incredibly, my book "Best stocks as of 7/15/2020" even beat SPY (the market), which have weighted a lot by the momentum stocks (FAANG for example). In the future and where appropriate, I may use an ETF that consists of the S&P500 stocks evenly weighted as a yardstick.
- No stock pickers including the well-known gurus have performed well consistently (such as Buffett in the last 10 years and Jessie Livermore). That's why I recommend stops to protect your portfolio.
- I have about 15 screens (selected from about 50 screens for this phase of the market). I only use the ones that have performed well recently. Most of my stocks are picked for safety and appreciation potential. A few may be picked for better appreciation at the expense of safety.

- There is no evergreen strategy. The market could irrational, unexpected events happen, and/or my strategies do not work in the current market. Consult your finance advisor before committing any money.

5   Newsletters and subscriptions

Why do you not see too many reviews on investment newsletters and subscriptions from the media? If it is a bad review, most likely they will not advertise in the media. If it is a good review, they may have to face legal actions in the future if the vendor's subscription or newsletter does not perform well.

I've been using investment newsletters / subscriptions for years. Many are priced reasonably and some are even free. While a lot of them are garbage, some are very good.

When you have a lot of money to invest and you're not using a financial adviser and/or not subscribing to any investment service, it could be a big financial mistake. You do not want to be penny smart but pound foolish. Very few have the knowledge and the time to make use of the free financial data, including the guidance and articles from the web.

You need a computer, access to the Internet and a spreadsheet in order to use most subscription services effectively.

I'm not going to compare specific services / newsletters at the risk of being sued, but I will include some general pointers on how to select them. Yesterday's garbage could be a gold mine today if the subscription improves and/or the market conditions fit what they recommend.

First, you need to find out your requirements and how much time you can afford to use them. If you have $20,000 or less to invest, most likely your investment both in time and money will not pay off; just buy an ETF and practice market timing described in this book. My pointers are:

- Newsletters giving you specific stocks to buy do not require much of your time. However, if they're successful, there will be too many followers buying the recommended stocks that can drive up the prices at least temporarily. The owner of the subscription service and his insiders will buy the recommended stocks before you unless they're not allowed to do so (but who's enforcing this?). I had several of these newsletters, and so far I have not renewed any one of them due to poor performance.

- If I found the Holy Grail of investing, do you believe I would share it with you for $100 or so? I only will after I invest my money first. My subscribers would push up the prices for me and then I could unload them before my subscribers.

  I am publishing a book (not a promise) in June time frame every year with the title "Best Stocks for 2021" recommending a handful of stocks. Due to my relatively small positions and few buyers of the book, it will not have the adverse effects described. Most of my recommendations should be value stocks for long term hold unless the market is risky. My books will not be the Holy Grail as my objective is beating the S&P 500 Index.

- If the volume of the recommended stocks are small, they can be manipulated easily either by the newsletter owners and/or by your peer subscribers. The first ones to sell the recommended stocks win and the last ones to sell them lose.

- I prefer systems that can find a lot of stocks by providing many searches (same as screens). However, it will take a lot of time to learn and test their performances unless they provide historical databases. Most likely, you need to further research each stock screened.

  From my experience, the best performance comes from the stocks that have been screened by more than one search especially for the short term (less than 6 months). My theory is that they've been identified by many folks and hence their prices could be jacked up. It is more profitable to buy them ahead of the herd and sell them before the herd. In any case, research the stock you are interested in.

- Most of you have received promotional mail that indicates their incredible performances such as tripling the money in a short time. Just ignore them. If it is that good, most likely they will keep it for themselves. It is the same for seminars that boost some penny stocks. Most likely the recommended stocks would rise initially to lure you and other suckers to move it. Watch out! As of 2016, I do not see these junk mail as often as before; the public is smarter. They must have switched their promotions to YouTube.

- A 'guru' told me that he made a big fortune in silver a month ago. Guess what? He also recommended selling it two months earlier and lost a lot of money in doing so. He is always right but he will not advertise the times he was wrong. We call it a double talk technique.

- There are free trial offers (or deeply discounted) for most subscription services. Take advantage of them. Some services require you to spend a lot of time, so ensure you have the time. Keep track of the performance yourself via paper trading. Do not trust their 'official' performances which can be manipulated.

- Subscribe to a newsletter that fits your style of investing. If you're a day trader, newsletters on long-term investing are not good for you. Some subscriptions handle all kinds of investing styles and you need to find the strategies and recommendations within the newsletter to fit your style. Short-term swing traders have different set of metrics than long-term investors.

- Newsletters on penny stocks are risky to most of us. They may show you a list of big winners but they do not show you their losers.

   I define penny stocks as the stock price less than $2 (officially $5) and a market cap less than 100 M. Once a long while I do trade penny stocks. Actually I bought ALU at $1 but ALU's market cap then was about 2 billion at the time. The stocks with prices between $1 and $10 represent the most volatile stocks but a few are real gems. They are routinely ignored by most analysts.

- There are many sectors like drugs, mines, insurance and banks that retail investors cannot evaluate them effectively. It is better to seek expert advice from specific newsletters. Check out their past performance and take advantage of the free trial offers.

- Remember there is no free lunch in life. The higher potential return of a stock, the riskier the stock is. To me, all trades are educated guesses. The more educated the guesses are, the higher chance they will perform in the long run. However, noting is 100% sure.

- Some newsletters / subscriptions save us time by summarizing the financial data by providing a value rank and a growth rank. Some provide a timely rank from the price momentum. When the market favors growth, use the growth rank, and vice versa.

- Be careful with the information from radio and TV commercials. Many try to sell to peoples' fear and greed by overstating without necessarily telling the whole story. It is not possible to make 50% in covered calls consistently or making another gold rush from $400 to $2,000. One advertises the market will lose 80% in 2016. It is possible but not likely. [Update: The market was profitable in 2016.] These are tactics to get you subscribing to their services.

- TV financial shows usually exaggerate in order to sell their products. Analyze them before you act on the news.

- As retail investors, most of us cannot afford to do extensive research. Many researches and market opinions are available on the internet free. Start to search for such information from your broker's site and financial sites such as SeekingAlpha.com, MarketWatch.com, CNNfn.com and Yahoo!Finance.com. Analyze the news and some could be obsolete, or could be manipulated with a hidden agenda.

- Most compare their performances with the S&P 500 index. Some investment newsletters inflate their performance with dividends while comparing to an index without including dividends.

  To illustrate, the S&P 500 has an average annual return of 1% on appreciation and 1.5% on dividends for a total return of 2.5%. Hence, the performance of a newsletter should compare itself to 2.5% not 1%.

- The performance of the last 10 years (I prefer the last 5 years) is more important than that of 25 years. The last 10 years is a better prediction of the newsletter than the last 25 years as the weatherman has found out.

  More than one time, I have found a popular subscription that did not beat S&P 500 in the last 5 years but it did in the last 20 years. It could be that too many folks are using the same strategy.

- When the new major researcher takes over the subscription, s/he may not have the same expertise as the previous researcher.

- Ensure the subscriptions change their strategies according to the current market conditions. For example, 10 years ago ADRs (U.S. listed stocks of foreign countries) performed far better than today.

The trend may reverse in the future.

- Few if any use real money for their portfolios, as they cannot cheat with real money. That's why you never achieve the compatible performance by following what the portfolio trades. Some can manipulate by using the best prices of the day. Some omit their losers. Do not trust any performance claims even from reputable monitor services unless the portfolios can be verified with real money.

  Some sample portfolios trade excessively and they may not fit your investment strategy.

- When a subscription service has several strategies (say 10 for illustration purposes), they will advertise the strategies with the best returns for a specific time period.

- On 12/8/2014 TNH was down by 12% by the end of the day. If they used the open price, it would have made a difference of 12%

Contrary to not recommending investment services, I recommend your broker for the stock research. AAII is a low-priced subscription, but Fidelity (requiring membership), Finviz and Yahoo!Finance are free today.

#Filler: My grandson

My six-year old grandson called the library about the availability of the book Mine Craft. The lady told him that only Mine Craft for Dummies was available. He told her it was not for him as he was not a dummy.

Filler: My favorite store

The new name of the merged companies "Family Dollar" and "Dollar Store" would be "General Family Dollar" or "Two Dollars Now".

If you want to prove the rich are more beautiful, just go to any dollar store. Must be offending a lot of folks. Sorry!

6 Advantages of a retail investor

The average retail investor does not beat the market due to switching between stocks and cash at the wrong time. Via the greed, they invest at the peak of the market and via fears they divest at the bottom. They do not expect the market to return from the bottom but it always does.

Most fund managers are smarter than I, better educated in investing than I, have ten times more research tools than I and have ten times more computer power than I. However, most of them do not beat me, the average casual retail investor. In addition, I spend less time in stock research than an average fund manager (most are working at least 60 hours a week). I hope the following help you to beat the market and the fund managers.

- They cannot beat the market all the time. When they do, more money flows in. It is very hard for them to perform with extraordinary cash. When the market is depressing, everyone cashes out their funds. They need to sell stocks even though they may have better potential to appreciate.

  The saying "When there is blood in the streets, most likely it is the best time to buy" is correct. 2009 is a recent example. Fund managers cannot take advantage of this opportunity as most clients have cashed out.

- Most cannot play market timing freely and they have to satisfy all the rules set up for the fund. Every time they trade a stock, they need to ensure no rules have been broken such as a restricted percent of a stock to the fund. Most funds prohibit their managers from shorting, buy contra ETFs and/or maintain high cash positions. Basically, most are not allowed to react to the market when it is going up or down.

- When they trade, their high volumes are easily tracked by day traders who can ride on their wagons. Hence they have to pay more to buy and get less to sell.

- By my rough estimate, they have about 1,000 stocks (about 600 for larger funds) to deal with. I as a retail investor have about 3,000 stocks even skipping most stocks with prices below $2 or not listed in the three major exchanges.

Their stocks have been fully evaluated by analysts and newsletters / subscriptions such as Value Line and /or some firms specializing in stock research for them. Hence, they do not gain any advantage by following their peers.

The small and mid-cap stocks are risky but are more rewarding statistically in the long run. Many fund managers cannot buy them due to the size of their funds.

o Their performance as a group is actually worse due to the closing down of non-performing funds.

o Not nimble enough.
By the time they have done all the research and received the approval to buy a specific stock, I may have bought the same stock already. Usually it takes at least a week for a large fund to complete trading a stock.

o The high expenses.
The fee is about 1.5% for the average fund. Most hedge funds charge even more with the average 2% for expenses plus 20% on the profit. When the fund and the broker belong to the same company, watch out on for how its brokerage arm makes more profitable. Most hedge funds have no penalty for losing your money, and hence it encourages their fund managers to take bigger risks.

o Not spending enough time to do their own research.
Many do not spend enough time on basic research and select the right strategies in current market conditions. They spend a lot of time in following the fund's and the company's objectives, rules and regulations.

o Wrong objective.
The objective of most funds is beating the common index after expenses. Most fund managers do not want to take too much risk and their personal objective is job security. One will not lose the job if his performance is similar to a target index. You achieve the same objective by buying an ETF that simulates the index for far lower expenses.

o The reason for some of their good performance is due to taking too much unnecessary risk and the high leverage. Their performance improves when the market is good, but degrades when the market is down. When I see the market is coming down, I would park more cash and I only use leverage when the market is going up.

- Retail investors have a lot of advantages over fund managers. However, I advise you not be day traders as beginners. Statistically most amateur traders lose money as they cannot compete with experienced, disciplined traders.

  However, discipline, knowledge and due diligence will make you money in the long term as a turtle investor.

Filler: Gamma rays

Gamma rays are the most effective tool for weight loss. If you die because of the gamma rays, you will lose weight gradually, naturally and surely

Filler: Victims?

We're victims of our own success: A higher living standard means higher wages, more protections for our workers and more regulations for our environment. All these will make us less competitive.

#Filler: How to end all our wars

If we send the children of our leaders to the front line, we will not have any wars.

The youths should enjoy the best time of their lives and not be sent back in body bags.

7   Hedge fund 101

LTCM (a hedge fund named Long Term Capital Management), with smart folks, ran their hedge funds into the ground. Many hedge funds are closed due to fraud, and/or poor performance.

The primary purpose is supposed to 'hedge' your investments from market plunges / dips. Since 2008, the government has printed so much money, and it make the market recover. It also make the hedges (shorts, derivatives, etc.) unnecessary. In reality, most hedge funds today do not hedge.

Hedge funds get tons of press coverage as a Holy Grail type of investing. The media need the advertising from this $2.5 trillion industry. It is similar to mutual funds, but they take more risk for supposedly better returns. Most require higher minimum investments and more restrictions such as requiring longer periods.

It could be the worst deal to most of their customers: 2% average up front and 20% average on your profit. It is more acceptable to me if the 20% is on profit over the S&P 500 return. Why should I pay you 20% on my 10% profit when the market rises by 15%? In this case, my fund loses 5% relative to the market.

Well, if they consistently make a lot of money for you, maybe it is not too much to object to. However, most risk your money by betting big recklessly. When they win, they get 20% of your profit and they use you for advertising to lure in other suckers. When they lose *your* money, they do not lose a penny. It encourages them to take big risks. I do not know any hedge fund (HF) manager who pays you back your losses.

You would have better return by investing in a no-load index fund, or a diversified ETF than an average hedge fund. To calculate the average hedge fund performance, you need to include the many hedge funds that are out of business. To illustrate my point, check out the performance of SPY in the last five years and that of the average hedge fund.

After a hedge fund has failed, most fund managers just open another hedge fund (if they do not go to jail first due to fraud) and give you all the excuse for losing your hard-earned money. Some lose their reputation, but you may not check them out their past performances.

In 2011, the hedge fund industry did not beat the S&P 500 index fund after their fees.

Some hedge fund managers learn [modern portfolio theories](#) from Ivy League universities and apply them in the hedge funds. Often their theories are based on wrong testing procedures, or they cannot be sustained in real life.

Many invest in new companies and small companies where they would have big profit swings. They need to learn the business of the company in which they plan to buy the stocks, interview the owners, read between the lines, and double check whether the owners are telling the truth by talking to their competitors, vendors and customers. It explains the high cost for their research. We just need to look at the transactions of the insiders. There is no need to travel to visit the company unless you want to.

Some use their specialties in certain sectors and that's fine. If they use derivatives, be careful and that's what resulted in our 2007 financial crisis. Derivatives could reduce the risk of the portfolio if they are properly used. If you still want to invest in them, ask for their methods and their historical performances. Very few hedge funds are good. When you find a good one, most likely it has been closed to new investors or its fees are outrageous.

The owner of a famous baseball franchise lost big money from a hedge fund that concentrated in the oil sector. Almost every ETF in this sector made good money that year, but he still stayed with the hedge fund and had similar miserable returns the following year. I did not blame him for his first mistake, but on his sticking with the same hedge fund after a losing year. It could be that the hedge fund gave him a hard time when he wanted to take his money out, or he could be busy in his baseball franchise.

One hedge fund has a performance of 25% every year over a long period of time. The SEC, takes notes and then investigates whether they were using insiders' information. It turned out it did. There are very few hedge funds with consistent performance beating the market after their hefty fees. If you find one, stay with them forever. One hedge fund was rated as the top fund and the next year it was out of business due to poor performance. Hedge fund managers chase after short-term returns as the outflow will be serious if they do not perform well. When they were successful recently, they had a hard time to perform with an excessive inflow of money.

In 1980, this industry started with really capable fund managers and made good money for their clients. After that, every analyst wanted to open a hedge fund and most did not even beat the market after their fees. Alternatively, just buy the ETF SPY (or similar ETF for the market) and relax, instead of waiting for the hedge fund to wipe out your savings. This industry is not properly regulated.

Do not believe in any articles / ads praising how great the hedge funds are without knowing their credibility and their hidden agendas. The hedge fund indexes usually ignore the survivor bias of the bankrupted hedge funds and the early exits of many hedge funds.

Since the hedge funds very seldom keep the stocks more than a year, their capital gains would be short-term and hence would be taxed at a higher rate than the long-term capital gains. In addition, many funds have a 1-3 year lock-up period and only allow withdrawals on the first day of each fiscal quarter.

Afterthoughts

- From WSJ, from 1999-2008, the hedge fund industry beats S&P 500 by 13% a year. From WSJ, from 2009 thru July 2012, it lagged the market by almost 8%.

    In 2011, the average hedge fund lost money when S&P 500 was flat. In 2012, the average hedge fund earned about 6% when S&P 500 was up 13%. It is 'genius' to buy an ETF representing the entire market instead of an average hedge fund.
- Now hedge funds can advertise.
A pig wearing lipstick is still a pig. If you run 5 hedge funds, you will advertise your best fund. Advertising industry will benefit and eventually their investors if hedge funds will pay for this expense.

    http://finance.fortune.cnn.com/2013/07/10/sec-votes-to-let-hedge-funds-advertise/?iid=HP_River
- A hedge fund article from SA.
http://seekingalpha.com/article/584861-hedge-funds-are-they-just-smooth-operators?source=kizur

- Another hedge fund fraud.
  http://money.cnn.com/2013/07/25/investing/sac-capital-charges/index.html?iid=HP_LN
- Gold even managed by a great hedge fund manager is down as of 7/2013.
  http://www.cnbc.com/id/100855708
- A famous hedge fund manager (so is the one on Sears) has big losses in JCP and shorting another company. It teaches us to diversify and be conservative.
  http://money.cnn.com/2013/08/26/investing/bill-ackman-sells-jcpenney/index.html?iid=HP_River
- In 50 years, the $10,000 investment will grow to $1,170,000 assuming a 10% return a year. However, about $700,000 will be the cost of the typical mutual fund. It will be better to buy an ETF (a far lower fee) and avoid market plunges described in my book.
- Hedge funds must have had a hard time in 2013. Hedging against a rising market is a fool's game. Another article to review.
- Many hedge funds and their investors lost serious money by shorting GameStop in 2021.

Links

LTCM: https://en.wikipedia.org/wiki/LongTerm_Capital_Management
Hedge Fund: http://en.wikipedia.org/wiki/Hedge_fund

Filler: Toaster and the economy
You can find many toasters made in the USA in museums. Is it OK to move the toaster factories from China to Vietnam?

The logic:
All toasters are made in China.
Chinese toasters are crappy.
Conclusion: All toasters are crappy.
Question: Do you find iPhone crappy (as it is assembled in China)?
Question: If we charge heavy tariffs on Chinese goods and the Chinese do the same on our exports such as Boeing planes (the disadvantage is to us if they do not have the same tariff on Airbuses). What is it called? Trade war.

Book 3: Simplest market timing

1   Simplest market timing

Why market timing
Before 2000, market timing was a waste of time. However after that, we have had two market plunges with the average loss of about 45%. It sounds harder to time the market than it actually is. We have a simple technique to detect market plunges and when to reenter the market. Our objective is reducing the loss to 25%.

Market timing depends on charts; the following describes how to use chart information without creating charts. Most charts will not identify the peaks and bottoms of the market as they depend on data (i.e. the stock prices). However, it would reduce further loses. It is simpler than it sounds. Just follow the procedure below.

The first part of this technique detects market plunges, and the second part advises you when to reenter the market. It applies to individual stocks too. It also works to detect the trend of a sector (entering an ETF for the specific sector instead of SPY) and a specific stock.

How to detect market plunges without charts (a.k.a. <u>Death Cross</u>)
1. Bring up Finviz.com.

2. Enter SPY (or any ETF that simulates the market) or RSP for equally weighed SPY.

3. If SMA-200% is positive, it indicates that the market plunge has not been detected and you can skip the following steps.

4. The market is plunging if SMA-50% is more negative than SMA-200%. To illustrate this condition, SMA-200% is -2% and SMA-50% is -5%.

5. Sell most stocks starting with the riskiest ones first such as the ones with negative earnings, high P/Es and/or high Debt/Equity. Obtain this info from Finviz.com by entering the symbol of the stock you own.

6. Conservative investors should sell only those over-priced stocks. Aggressive investors should sell all stocks. Extremely aggressive investors should sell all stocks, buy contra ETFs, and even short stocks. I do not recommend beginners to be aggressive.

When to return to the market (a.k.a. Golden Cross)

Use the above in a reversed sense to detect whether the market has been recovering. However, when the SMA-200% turns positive, I would start buying value stocks (low P/E but the 'E' has to be positive, and/or low Debt/Equity).

1. Bring up Finviz.com.

2. Enter SPY (or any ETF that simulates the market).

3. If SMA-200% is negative, the market is not recovering, and you can skip the following steps.

4. Sell all contra ETFs and close all shorts if you have any.

5. Market recovery is confirmed when SMA-50% is more positive than SMA-200%. To illustrate this condition, SMA-200% is 2% and SMA-50% is 5%. Commit a large percent of cash (or all cash for aggressive investors) to stocks. If you do not know what to buy, buy SPY or an ETF that simulates the market.

How often to check the market timing indicators
Do the above once a month. When the SPY price is closer to SMA actions percentage, perform the above once a week. The charts and data for market timing described in this book are based on SMA-350 (Simple Moving Average) that is more preferable than this simple procedure, but it requires some simple charting.

Nothing is perfect
If the market timing is perfect, there would be no poor folks. The major 'defects' are:
- It does not detect the peak / bottom as it depends on past data. However, it would save you a lot during the crash.
- It is hard to determine whether it is a correction or a crash.
- From 2000 to 2010, there is only one false signal. The indicator tells you to exit and then tell you reenter the market shortly. In most cases, you do not lose a lot. After 2010, we have more false signals.
- The market may not be rational or may be influenced due to specific conditions such as excessive printing of USD. If you do not mind charting, use SMA 350 (or 400) using SPY. Buy when the price is above SMA-350 (or SMA-400), and sell otherwise. SMA-400 reduces the number of false signals but not nimble.

2   The power of market timing

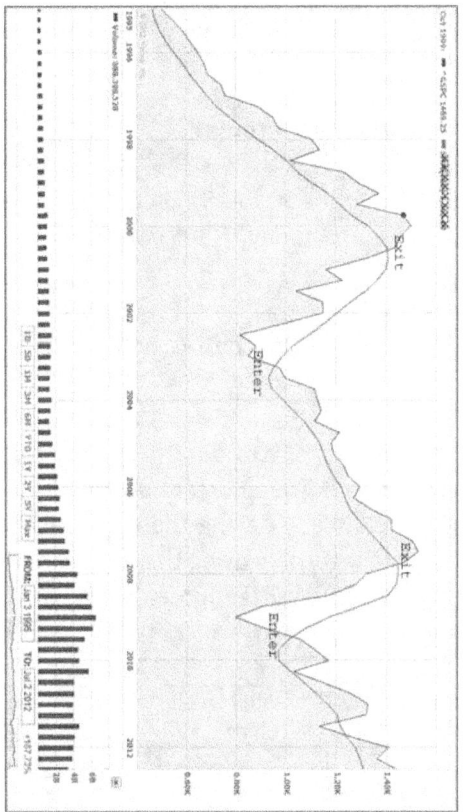

Most e-book readers allow you to select the graph to make it fit entirely on your screen. I use SPY, an ETF simulating the market. Detecting market plunges as seen in this graph indicates the exit points and reentry points also from 2000 to 9-2009 as follows.

Market Plunge	Peak	Bottom	Indicator Exit	Indicator Reenter
2000	08/28/00	09/20/02	10/01/00	06/01/03
2007	10/12/07	03/06/09	02/01/08	09/01/09
			08/01/11	11/01/11

Table: Vital Dates

For simplicity I skipped a few brief exits and reentries since 2011. You can run the simple chart once a month. When it indicates a potential market plunge is close, run the chart once a week. The last row represents a false signal.

This is based on stock prices so it may not identify the peaks and bottoms precisely, but so far it has not failed to avoid big losses and ensure big gains by reentering the market. I hope the next market plunge would give us enough time to act as these two did.

Unbelievable return with market timing

Calculate how much you made if you followed the above exit points and reenter points from 2000 to today. I bet you would have made a good fortune.

I compared the above returns with the SPY without market timing from 1-2000 to 9-2013.

There are many assumptions. Dividends and compounding are not considered. My return should be substantially better if I include buying contra ETFs during the exits and selling them during the reentries. I was shocked by the incredible return by using this simple market timing. Again, past performance does not guarantee future performances.

Summary info:

S&P 500 1-2000 to 9-2013	With Market Timing	Without Market Timing
Better	500%	
Gain	1,000	167
Gain %	68%	11%
Annualized gained	5%	1%
Days	4,959	4,959

Calculations:

S & P 500	With Market Timing	Without Market Timing
1-2000	1,469[1]	1,469[1]
Exit 10/01/00	1,041[2]	1,041
Enter 06/01/03	1,041	964[4]
Exit 02/01/08	1,489[3]	1,379[4]
Enter 09/01/09	1489	1,020[5]
Exit 08/01/11	1,888	1,293
Enter 11/01/11	1,888	1,251
09/03/13	2,469	1.638
Gained	2,469 – 1,469=1,000	1,638-1,469=167
Gain %	1000/1469 = 68%	167/1469 = 11%
Annualized gained	68% * 365/4959=5%	11%*365/4959=1%
Better	(1,000-167)/167 = 500%	

Portfolio with Market Timing:

[1] Both start with S&P 500 of 1,469 on 1-3-2000.

[2] 10/01/00
The market timing portfolio exits the market and remains the same value of 1,041 until 6/1/00.

[3] 02/01/08
The market timing portfolio exits the market and remains the same value of 1,489 until 9/1/09.

'1,489' is calculated as follows:
1,041 * (1 + Rate) = 1,041 * (1 + 1,379-964)/964) = 1,489
where the S&P 500 is 964 on 6/1/00 and 1,379 on 2/1/08.

The other calculations are based on the S&P 500 at 1,020 on 9/1/9, 1,293 on 8/1/11, 1,251 on 11/1/11 and 1,636 on 9/3/13.

Portfolio without Market Timing:

[1] Both starts with the S&P 500 of 1,469 on 1-3-2000. We could use the 9/3/13 the S&P 500 value, but it would not account for some compounded interest considerations.

[4] S&P 500 is 964 on 6/1/00 and 1,379 on 2/1/08.

[5] 02/01/08. The portfolio value is calculated to be 1,020 as follows:
1,379 * (1 + Rate) = 1,379 * (1 + (1020-1379)/1379) = 1,020
where S&P 500 is 1,379 on 2/1/08 and 1,020 on 9/1/09.

The other calculations are based on the S&P 500 at 1,293 on 8/1/11, 1,251 on 11/1/11 and 1,636 on 9/3/13.

I cannot believe the shocking return with market timing. I checked my calculations and there was nothing wrong that I could find. If you find something wrong, send your findings to me (pow_tony@yahoo.com).

Even if I made a mistake somehow and got 100% instead of 500%, it still doubles the return without market timing! Ask any fund manager what it means to his or her fund performance and his / her career.

3   Bubbles

Bubbles have existed throughout our history. Bubbles occur due to the excessive valuation most likely driven up by the big institutional investors (fund managers, pension managers, hedge fund manager, etc.). Asset valuations are then driven even higher by the retail investors. For example in 3/2014, the market bubble was caused by the government stimulus with the injection of capital into the excessive money supply and subsidies. The first investors riding the wave made good money, and the last ones buying at the peak would lose.

From our recent history, we have the 2000 internet bubble, and then the 2007 (2008 for some) housing bubble. The chapter "Spotting Big Market Plunges" illustrates it was easy to detect the last two plunges. It could save us more than 25% of your portfolio in the next plunge.

Today most of the mentioned bubbles could be caused by pumping too much money into the economy by the government. However, the government cannot keep on injecting money into the economy, and ask our children to pay for our debts forever. When the injections stop, the market will drop fast and deep.

USD
As of mid-2020, the USD is doing quite well. It could be the other countries (EU and Japan) that are doing worse off than us, as Einstein said, "everything is relative". The strong USD is not good for exports and the global corporations would have less profits after converting them back to USD. However, the excessive printing of money and high government debts would shake the status of USD as a reserve currency. It will also be hurt if China sells the U.S. Treasury bonds which she owns.

Bond
The bond bubble will burst when the interest rates rise. Also it will as the interest rates should have bottomed by mid-2020. It is even possible that it could go negative.

Stocks

There are several bubble stocks such as FAANGs. The market was peaking in Jan., 2020 before the virus breakout. Play defense with your stop loss orders. The record of margin debt is a big concern. When the credit is tightened with higher interest rates, this bubble will burst.

When to act

Without a time machine, no one can pin point when most of these bubbles will burst. Your market timing depends on your risk tolerance, your knowledge and your greed.

Today, we have the housing bubble (2007-2008), the gold bubble, the market bubble, the second housing bubble, the debt bubble, the bond bubble, the second market bubble, etc. It seems like we can never get out of the bubble cycle. In 2020, the world would be in a global recession if the trade war between the two largest economies continue. It would be worse for sure, if the trade war turns into a military war.

The world is economically connected better than before. When the U.S.A. sneezes, it affects our trading partners such as European countries along with China and Japan, and also their partners such as the resource-rich countries of S. America, Australia, Russia, Canada and Africa.

For me, it is safer not to try to make the last buck when the reward / risk ratio is too low. A good sleep would improve your health which is worth all the gold in the world.

4 Actions for different stages of a market cycle

There are different strategies for the different stages of the market cycle.

Strategies during market plunges

The market plunge is defined as the period between the market peak and the market bottom. It usually lasts for one year or two.

When you spot the potential plunge, consider the following actions. It depends on your risk tolerance and your investment style.

1. Contrary to popular belief, parking cash is a strategy too. Cash is needed later to move back to equities.

2. Be conservative: Buy stocks based on value and not based on momentum. Reduce your new purchases and take profits especially on momentum stocks. I buy one stock for every two or three stocks I sold during this stage.

3. Protect your portfolio with stop orders. It is one of the few times I recommend stop orders. If you watch the market every day, just place market orders when your stock falls to a specific price.

4. Buy contra ETFs for aggressive investors.

5. Sell cover calls. I prefer to sell the stocks I own.

6. Older folks may not want to sell the stocks with huge gains (due to tax consideration) or stocks that give them income stream of dividends. They can use options to protect potential losses for the stocks they own.

What to do after the plunge

In the first year after the start of the plunge, do not start to buy unless they are very good values. Aggressive investors should start closing their short positions/put options and selling contra ETFs.

When the market plunges, it usually takes at least one year to recover as investors believe they have to sell to protect their remaining nest eggs. Those sectors that cause the bubble will take even longer to recover.

After the plunge, watch out for the interest rate. If it is still high, it is the best time to buy high-yield bonds (i.e. junk bonds). Ensure that the corporation issuing the bonds would not bankrupt; the bonds from the old GM in 2007 lost most of their values. They will appreciate when the interest rates drops that the government would routinely do to stimulate the economy. 2008 is not a good year to invest in stocks and bonds except the contra ETFs and selling shorts, but 2009 definitely is (it is my Early Recovery phase of the market cycle).

Personally I prefer not to buy any stocks until the chart tells us to reenter the market. It is the fear that investors do not want to reenter the market. The market will always recover as in the past history.

Even before the recovery, some sectors (called consumer staple) are doing better such as health care, foodstuffs, utilities and pharmaceuticals that are always in demand. Interest-sensitive sectors such as housing and auto will suffer disproportionately. They are also called cyclical stocks. Consumer Discretionary are sectors that suffer a lot in a recession such as high tech products.

What to do in early recovery and after

When the market is starting to recovery (2003 and 2009 in the last two market cycles), the potential profit is the highest. Buy deeply-valued stocks on companies that have been beaten down. They will recover with the highest appreciation potential. I call it the bottom fishing strategy.

Larger companies are fishing too to acquire smaller companies that fit into their corporate synergy or small companies with the technology and/or the customer base they need.

Valued stocks could be defined a little differently in this phase. Many times P/E is not a good metric as most companies are losing money. 2003 is such a year. If you expect the recession will end in 2 years and the company has enough cash to survive in two years based on its annual burn rate, then it would be a buy candidate.

In both 2003 and 2009, I spotted at least one company that was acquired by a larger company. From my memory, one company in 2003 was acquired by IBM giving me more than 2 times return. In 2009, at least three companies were acquired giving me an average annualized return of over 200%.

Momentum strategy rewards us best from the end of the early recovery phase to the peak phase. The up phase started in 2004 for 2000 market cycle and 2010 in the 2007 market cycle.

Note. The parameters of SMA-200, SMA-350, SMA-90, etc. and RSI are different for market exit/reentry, correction exit and individual stocks. These are the guidelines only. Stocks are more volatile than the market and are very different among them. Hence, define the 'days' according to the historical pattern of the individual stock and how often you trade them.

Filler: My translation from my Chinese friend's poem

When you understand "everything is changing", you won't be boosting your achievements. Today's splendid life could be a mess tomorrow.

When you understand "everything is changing", you won't be sad. Today's gloom could turn into sunshine tomorrow.

When you understand "everything is changing", you know today's gain could be tomorrow's loss and vice versa.

When you understand "everything is changing", there is no need to react to today's loss, gain, happiness and sadness.

8   A non-correlation of the market and business

The Business Cycle (same as the Economic Cycle) is supposed to lag the Market Cycle[1] by about 6 months as the stock market is a leading indicator of the economy. As of May of 2013, this has not occurred. The U.S. economy does not correlate to the stock market. It seldom happens. The market has recovered most of its losses from 2007-2008 and actually is making new heights.

The economy is still in a recession considering the high unemployment / under-employment and the poor GDP growth. The global economies are more inter-connected than before, and our trade partners are also not doing well. Though there have been some recent signs of recovery in the U.S. economy, the job employment may never reach its previous peak. As of 3/2016, the non-correlation continues.

Is this non-correlation important to us, the retail investors?

For an economist, the Economic Cycle is important. For an investor, the Market Cycle is important. Economists forecast business growth, GDP growth, job growth, housing start, etc., and plan accordingly. Investors care about the potential appreciation of their portfolios.

It could be the beginning of this non-correlation for the coming decade. There is a good chance economists can no longer depend on the previous correlation to use the market to predict the economy at least for a while. As long as the market is moving up, investors are not concerned with the non-correlation.

However, most likely the market will correlate again in the future with the economy as there has always been a correlation as far as I can remember. Until the following reasons of this non-correlation change, the correlation will continue.

The reasons for this non-correlation

1. Most big companies are now global companies.
   Hiring at these multinational corporations (MNCs) depends on where the offer is for the greatest benefits including low workforce salary, educated workers, tax credits, less taxes, stable government, good infrastructure, etc. A good portion of MNCs' incomes are from foreign countries. Hence the U.S. market is getting less correlated with the U.S. economy which uses local employment as a measurement.

2. Too many government interventions.
   The government bailed out too many companies that should fail. No companies are too big to fail. It has not punished the executives/bankers to get us into this recession thru their greed. The market may falsely expect that future failing companies will be bailed out. Hence, the stock market is expected to be protected by the government.

3. There is still a lot of easy money.
   Since the recession, banks are flooded with government money to invest. They loan out money to investors instead of loaning it to small businesses and house buyers to stimulate the economy. In addition,

the demands from businesses and potential house buyers have been reduced. The cash reserves if not loaned out must be very high.

Corporations now have the highest cash reserves for a long while. They use their cash reserves to buy back their own stocks, acquire companies and increase dividends. All these actions increase their stock values. Dividend stocks are flocked by income seekers especially with low bond yields.

When the government borrows a lot of money (to the ceiling literally), everything including the market looks good. However, somehow and sometime the taxpayers will pay for those debts to China, Japan and whatever other treasury buyers. Today the U.S. has a benefit: It will repay the debtors with depreciated dollars (not true if 2016).

A country loses its competitive edge if a good percentage of the GDP is used for servicing those debts. If the USA were a company that could not service its debts, it would be bankrupt. Most believe this is the primary reason.

4. Government regulations typically do not help the economy. To illustrate, the expected ObamaCare is discouraging small businesses from hiring.

5. Today's market may not be a good indicator of its value, if this were considered to be a commodity unit (a combination of natural resources including gold) instead of the USD.

6. There are too many factors that influence both the market and the economy in separate directions. Examples include the recent shale energy discovery which could improve the economy. A new war would do the opposite.

What should be done

1. The government cannot pump that much cash into the economy.

    Depreciating our currency is a short-term solution at best as it would improve our trade both ways. The status of being a reserve currency is shaken.

2. The United States government must address how to service its debt! The high debt will deteriorate the United States' competitive edge in the global markets. A high percentage of our GDP to service the debts will not help the economy.

3. We and the government need to bite the bullet with more taxes, more incentives to create jobs, less entitlements, less welfare... Ending the current two wars and avoiding future wars are almost mandatory to improve the economy.

4. The U.S. economy cannot be recovered without job recovery. The money spent in creating jobs will be better spent than on welfare and unemployment benefits. Hiring more government employees is the problem, not a solution.

Conclusion

It may be better to invest in a rising market than holding the depreciating cash. However, this non-correlation will not continue forever. The basic reason that stock appreciates is the company's ability to improve its earning. P/E is still the best yardstick on how fairly a company stock is priced. With a fixed 'E' for example and a rising 'P', the company's stock will be over-priced and will return to its average value (the average P/E for the last five years).

The correlation will be back again in a matter of time.

Footnote

[1]The market can only act as a leading indicator or proxy of economic activity if there is consensus on the direction. Sometimes what is coming in six months is fairly predictable but at other times when pundits are at odds the future course is fuzzy. So market indices are really tracking where consensus "thinks" GDP is going'.

To be clear a market index is a summary of where consensus believes the economy is headed and this sentiment is a proxy for forward earnings. For the playing stocks and not the index, it is their cumulative sentiment which acts as a guide.

Afterthoughts

- There are many other correlations. The following should correlate with the economy: construction industry, employment, commodity /commodity-related currency and oil. Once a while and for a good reason, they do not.
- QE, printing money, foreign loans (to China...), reserve currency, debt ceiling all mean the same: Live in a higher standard of living than we can afford.

  When Uncle Sam unsuccessfully uses all the tools to maintain our living standard and being the world's policeman, he runs out of tools. That will build a higher cliff for us to fall. Hopefully the shale energy will save our economy.
- The global economy still has not recovered as of July, 2013 according to this article.
(http://www.telegraph.co.uk/finance/economics/10174862/Renewed-fear-of-global-recession-as-companies-rein-in-spending-plans.html)
- Here are some economic indicators.
  http://en.wikipedia.org/wiki/Economic_indicator
- This time is REALLY different. Your Dad's generation does not have internet, powerful PC, low-interest commission, trading at a click of the mouse... Global economies are better connected via internet, shipping... All these affect our lives and economies.
- As of 09/2020, the market is making new heights. It could be the riskiest time and many predicated the market would crash after the election. Buy defensive stocks as Buffett was doing in this time frame.

Link: Making money during a crash.
https://www.youtube.com/watch?v=DjDCg4750dw

Sectors for market stages:
https://www.youtube.com/watch?v=FRdeXgf0rN8

#Filler: Do not speculate
Many speculators made big and then lost it all. There are many examples from the hedge funds.
Do not use leverage too much including the leveraged ETFs and margin accounts.

Do time the market in a logical way. Stay in the market as we have more bullish years than bearish years if you do not time the market.

5 Market timing by calendar

The following predictions are based on historical data. You may have slightly different findings depending on when you start and when you end your testing.

You can load the historical data of SPY via Yahoo!Finance and check out how close you are or different from my own predictions. They are my predictions based on historical data. Use it as a reference only.

- Presidential cycle.
  Usually the market performs worse in the first two years after the election than the next two. During the **3rd year** the president has to make the economy look rosy in order to buy votes. Statistically it is the best year for the market and is followed by a good year (the election year). The government may stimulate the economy, the stock market and employment by printing more money, lowering interest rates and lowering taxes. The market in the 100 days before the election should be positive and less volatile according to 40 years of data. The next 100 days after the inauguration should be good for the market (termed as the honeymoon period).

  Democratic presidents have better market performance statistically than Republican presidents. This is not too logical as though Republicans are more pro-business traditionally.

- Olympics.
  It has been proven that the host country has a better chance that its stock market appreciates the year after the Olympics. It could be due to the exposure from the Olympics and / or the huge expenses in preparing for the Olympics.

  The last two Olympics follow this pattern as of 12/23/2013:

Olympics Country / Year	ETF	Period	Return
United Kingdom / 2012	EWU	Jan. 3, 2013 - Dec. 23, 2013	11%
China / 2008	FXI	Jan. 3, 2009 - Dec. 31, 2009	43%

  Greece could be an exception. It is too small a country to host this world-class event and it has wasted too many resources by building too many white elephants that the country can never justify. Brazil depends on its export of natural resources to China, so I do not count on the Olympics effect there.

Winning a lot of Olympic medals has no prediction for the stock markets. Both the Russian Empire and E. Germany were winners but disappeared in their original forms afterwards.

- Seasonal.
  Best profitable investment period is: Nov. 1 to April 30 of the following year. It is similar to the saying 'Sell in May and Go away'. It did not work since 2009 as it was an Early Recovery (defined by me) in the market cycle.

  The market does not always happen as predicted. However, when more folks follow this, it becomes a self-fulfilling prophecy. I prefer "Sell on April 15 and come back on Oct. 15" to act before the herd. The more practical strategy is to start selling in April 1 and become more aggressive (selling at closer to the market prices) when it is close to May 1. For the last five years, I did not find this prediction reliable.

  The explanation of the 'summer doldrums' could be that the investors cash their stocks for vacations and college tuition in the fall. Buying quality companies at the dips could be profitable.

- The worst month: September.
  The next worst month is October. However, if there is no serious market crash during October (and this month has more than its shares of crashes), it could be the best month to buy stocks.

- The best month for the bull: November.
  However, several market bottoms occurred in October and November. The next strong month is December.

- Best 30 days: Dec. 15 to Jan. 15, next year.
  It was correct for the period of 2012-2013.

- Window dressing.
  Institutional investors sell their losers and buy winners around Nov. 1. From my rough estimate and on the average, the winners have a 2% percentage point gain better than the market and the losers have 1% worse than the market.

I recommend that you evaluate the top 10 winners from the last 10 months or YTD in Oct. 15 and sell them at 3% gain or two months later.

I recommend that you buy in Dec. and sell them 3 months later. Include the stocks with more than 30% loss for the last 11 months or YTD, sort them by Earning Yield in descending order and evaluate the top 10 stocks.

In both cases, do not buy foreign stocks and stocks with return of capital. Ignore stocks not in the three major exchanges, with low volumes and stock prices less than $2. Do not buy in losing years such as 2007 and 2008. I have my tests with my own assumptions and I use tools not available to most readers.

This is a guideline only. Do not buy any stocks during market plunges. Current events should be considered first such as a potential war and the hiking of interest rates.

Afterthoughts

- I predict it will be a sideways market in the later part of 2013. I am following the sideways strategy: Buy on dips and sell when the market is ups. One's prediction.

- Why September has a bad reputation?
  http://www.marketwatch.com/story/betting-on-septembers-terrible-odds-2013-08-27?dist=beforebell

  The September of 2013 (2 days away at the time of this writing) will have more problems. Check it out how many of the following are correct on Oc. 1, 2013. Use it as a future guideline to predict the next September using the current market conditions then:

  1. The market is not excessively expensive, but it is not cheap. It is due for a 5% correction.
  2. Unrest in Syria (check any unrest in your next prediction on September).
  3. High oil prices due to Syria.
  4. September is statistically a bad month for the stock market. However, it could be an opportunity to invest after the correction if any.
  5. Interest rates is rising.

6. All the above indicate the market will dip. However, the rosier outlook is that the global economies are improving even slowly.

- January effect.
  The performance of January may determine how the entire year performs. I cannot find any rationale but it has been proven right statistically.

- Earnings period announced in Jan., April, July and Oct. would cause big swings in stocks when they have surprises. Earning revisions could be a good predictor.
  http://www.investopedia.com/terms/e/earningsseason.asp

Links
Presidential Cycle:
http://www.investopedia.com/articles/financial-theory/08/presidential-election-cycle.asp

Calendar-based market timing:
http://stock-chartist.com/2010/10/calendar-based-market-timing/

Calendar market timing for 2013:
http://www.investorecho.com/archives/8047

Filler: Fidelity
From Fidelity.com, click on "News & Research" and then "Stock Market & Sector Performance" for Equity Market Commentary.
#Filler: False alarm
From 2000 to 2010, there is only one false alarm. From 2011 to 2016, there are more false alarms. We can change the parameter from SMA-350 to SMA-400 to reduce the number of false alarms at the expense of detecting the plunge a little late. The market before 2000 is quite different from the market today. Hence, I do not use the data before 2000.

6 Summary of investment calendar

I made the following charts so it is easier to time the market by the calendar.

All dates are inclusive.

No.	Metric		Score
1	Seasonal	Nov. - April, Score = 1	
2	Best Month	Nov., Score = 1	
		Sep., Score = -1	
3	Best Days	Dec. 15 – Jan.15 Score = 1	
4	Presidential Cycle	Election Year, Score = 1	
		1st Year in Office, Score = -1	
		2nd year, Score = -1	
		3rd year, Score = 2	
5	Presidential[3]	Democratic = 1 Republican = -1	
6	Market Cycle	Early Recovery, Score = 3	
		Up, Score = 2	
		Peak, Score = 1	
7	SPY (Finviz.com)	SMA200% > 8%[2] Score = -1	
		SMA200% < 0 Score = -1	
		RSI(14) > 65% Score = -1	
		Grand Score	

Footnote.
1. Refer to Market Cycle chapter on how I define phases of a cycle.
2. For simplicity, use Finviz.com. Enter SPY and you will find SMA200% and RSI(14) to predict whether the market is peaking and overbought.
3. I'm political neutral. The selection is based on historical statistics.

Add up all the scores. The passing grade is 0. According to my table which is based on my personal selections/preferences, the market is favorable when the grand score is 1 or higher. I bet it is the first time you see such a scoring system for market timing.

Sectors for market cycle

Market Phase[1]	Favorable	Unfavorable
Early Recovery	Financial, Technology, Industrial	Energy, Telecom, Utilities
Up	Technology, Industrial	
Peak	Mineral, Health Care, Energy	
Bottom	Consumer Staples, Utilities	Consumer Discretionary, Technology, Industrial

Seasonal	Favorable	Unfavorable
Winter	Energy, Utilities	
End of year	QQQ, EWG	
Olympics	ETF for host country[2]	

Footnote.
1 Refer to Market Cycle chapter on how I define phases of a cycle.
2 Buy it next year after the Olympics. It could be due to higher GDP or the publicity. However, be selective. Greece is too small a country to host an Olympics.

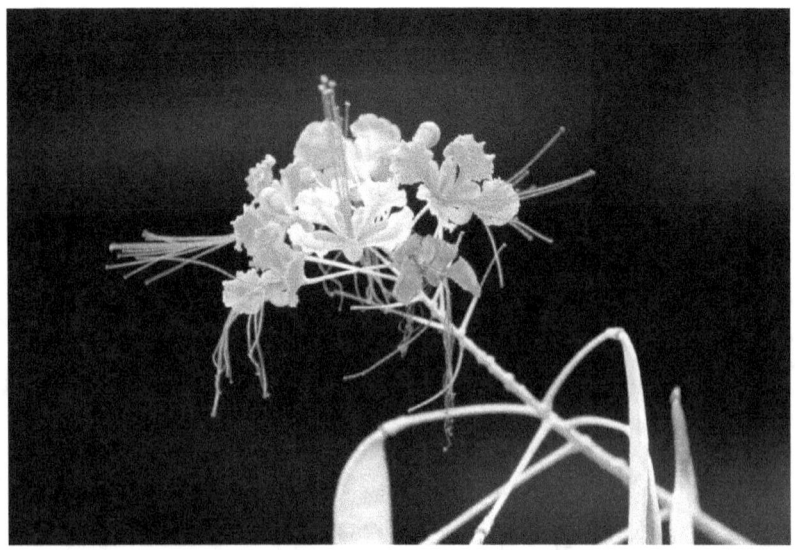

Book 4: Evaluate ETFs

1   Quick analysis of ETFs

Evaluate an ETF

ETFs are a basket of stocks according to the market, a specific sector, country or a specific theme.

Yahoo!Finance used to give the P/E of an ETF. Try to get it from ETFdb.com. Enter the symbol of the ETF such as XLU, and then select Valuation. If it is below 15 and above zero, it could be a value ETF. Also, if the current price is lower than its NAV, it is sold at a discount (or premium vice versa). Compare its YTD Return to SPY's.

Alternatively, get similar info from http://www.multpl.com/. In addition, this web site provides the following metrics: Shiller P/E, Price/Sales, and Price/Book.

From Finviz.com, enter the ETF symbol. If SMA-20%, SMA-50% and SMA-200% are all positive, most likely the ETF is in an uptrend. To illustrate, SMA-200 is Simple Moving Average for the last 200 trading sessions (no trading on weekends and specific holidays). The percent is how much the stock price of the ETF is above the SMA. If the percent is negative, it means the stock price is below the SMA.

If your average holding period of your stocks is about 50 days, SMA-50% is more appropriate to you.

If RSI(14) > 65, it is probably over-sold; if it is < 30, it is probably under-sold (indicating value).

In addition, ensure the ETF's average volume is high (I suggest more than 10,000 shares), the market cap is more than 300 M, and it has low fees. Most popular ETFs have these characteristics. Beginners should avoid leveraged ETFs.

How to determine if the sector has been recovered

It is easier to profit by following the uptrend of an ETF using the above info. It is hard to detect when the bottom of an ETF has been reached. If SMA-20%, SMA-50% and SMA-200% are all positive, most likely the ETF is in an uptrend or it has recovered. It does not always happen as predicted, so use stops to protect your investment.

An example
First, determine whether the market is risky. Most beginners should not invest in a risky market. Advanced investors can bet against the market or a specific sector by buying contra ETFs or puts.

Next, you want to limit the number of sector ETFs by selecting those that are either in an uptrend or hitting bottom (bottom is hard to predict). Personally I prefer sectors with long-term uptrends (indicated by articles found in many web sites including cnnfn.com and Seeking Alpha.

For illustration purposes only for deteriorating market conditions, I would select the following ETFs: SPY (simulating the market based on large companies) and XLP (consumer staples). XLP should perform better than XLY (consumer discretionary) during a recession as those products are the necessities.

Technical indicators such as SMA-50 (Simple Moving Average for the last 50 sessions), SMA-200 and RSI(14) are obtained from Finviz.com and the rest are obtained from Yahoo!Finance.com. After you buy the ETF, use a stop loss to protect your investment. For example, bio tech sector moved up for many months until it crashed in 2015. Change the stop loss value every month to protect your gains in this case.

As of 2/5/2016	SPY	XLP (staples)	XLY (discret.)
Price	190	50	71
NAV	192	50	73
• Technical			
SMA-50	-4%	0%	-7%
SMA-200	-6%	2%	-7%
RSI(14)	44	50	36
Other	Double bottom at $186		
• Fundamental			
P/E	17	20	19
Yield	2.1%	2.5%	1.5%
YTD return	-5%	0.5%	-5%
Net asset	174 B	9 B	10 B

Explanation
- The figures may not be identical among web sites due to the dates they are using.

- XLY has best discount among the 3 ETFs as most investors believe a recession is coming.
- XLP has less down trend among the 3 ETFs as expected.
- XLY is more undersold among the three as expected.
- Double bottom is a technical pattern that indicates the stock would surge upward.
- SPY has a better value according to its P/E.
- XLY's dividend is the least among the three as they have more tech companies in the ETF. They have to plow back the profits to research and development.
- XLP has the best YTD return among the three.
- As long as the asset is above 500 M (200 M for specialized ETFs), it is fine and all three pass this mark.

There are many metrics such as Debt/Equity not readily available from most web sites. Many sites list the top holdings of a specific ETF. Just average the metrics of the top ten or so of its stock holdings.

#Filler: Illogical logic

If we do not test for the pandemic, we would have zero increase in this pandemic. Some silly folks buy this argument. What happens to the once-great country?

Filler: The problems of the U.S.

1. Our political system. We waste time arguing between the two parties. There is no long-term planning, as the other party could claim the credit. Same as corporations' CEOs who care about their yearly bonuses.
2. The politicians have to satisfy their voters. Today give them free cash by jacking up the printing press. And ignore the long-term consequences.
3. We have to protect our workers, our environment... Hence, we cannot compete with many countries.
4. We have spent too much on military and ignore our crumpling infrastructure.
5. Historically no country can rule the world forever.
6. We blame China, but ignore how hard working Chinese are.

2   An example

This example evaluates RING, a gold miner, using ETFdb and Finviz that are free from the web. The data is from July, 6, 2020.

Bring up ETFdb and enter RING in the search. There are basic info that are important to me: Sector (gold miners), Asset Size (Large-Cap), Issuer (iShares), Inception (Jan. 31, 2012), Expense Ratio (0.39%) and Tax Form (1099).

They fit all my requirements. The expense ratio is higher than most ETFs that simulating an index such as SPY. I try to trade ETFs using Tax Form 1099 in my taxable accounts. The large cap created about 8 years ago by a reputable company are good.

Select "Dividend and Valuation". P/E of 17.39 is fine in a rank of 11 in 27 in similar group of ETFs. As in my books, I stated it is hard to evaluate miners. I buy this ETF primarily to fight the possibility of inflation and the potential depreciation of USD. The dividend rate of 0.52% (0.70% from Finviz) is in the low range of the scale; it is fine for me as dividend is not my concern.

There are more info from this web site. For simplicity, bring up Finviz:
- The short-term trend is up (SMA-20% = 8% and SMA-50% = 7%).
- The long-term trend is up (SMA-200% = 26%).
- It is close to overbought (RSI(14) = 64%; 65% to me is overbought).
- It is -4% from 52-w High. It has performed well from the YTD, Last Year, Last Quarter, Last Month and Last Week.
- It almost doubles in price from mid-March this year.
- Avg. Vol. is fine.

From ETFdb, check the Holding. It has 39 stocks, so it is quite diversified for this industry. The two top holdings are NEM (19%) and ABX (18%), which is listed as GOLD in NYSX. I also consider to buy these two stocks in addition to RING. You can estimate the other metrics that are not available by averaging these two stocks. Here is my summary:

STOCK	NEM	GOLD
Forward P/E	20	25
Debt / Share	0.31	0.24
ROE	17%	22%
Sales Q/Q	43%	30%
EPS Q/Q	389%	254%
SMA50	2%	4%
RSI(14)	59%	60%
Insider Trans	-13%	N/A
Fidelity's Equity Summary Score	6.1	6.8

3   ETFs / Mutual Funds

What is an ETF

ETFs have basic differences from mutual funds: 1. Lower management expenses, 2. Trade ETFs same as stocks, and 3. Usually more diversified but not more selective than the related mutual funds such as NOBL vs FRDPX.

The major classifications of ETFs are 1. Simulating an index such as SPY, QQQ and DIA, 2. Simulating a sector such as XLE and SOXX, 3. Simulating an asset class such as GLD and SLV, 4. Simulating a country or a group of countries such as EWC and FXI, 5. Managed by a manager(s) such as ARKK, 6. Betting a market or sector to go down such as SH and PSQ, and 7. Leveraged (not recommended for beginners).

Fidelity: Index ETFs (https://www.fidelity.com/etfs/overview).

Wikipedia on ETF (http://en.wikipedia.org/wiki/Exchange-traded_fund).

List of ETFs

ETF data base (Recommended): http://etfdb.com/
ETF Bloomberg: http://www.bloomberg.com/markets/etfs/
ETF Trends: http://www.etftrends.com/
A list of ETFs. Seeking Alpha.
http://etf.stock-encyclopedia.com/category/)
A list of contra ETFs (or bear ETFs)
http://www.tradermike.net/inverse-short-etfs-bearish-etf-funds/
Misc.: ETFGuide, ETFReplay

Fidelity low-cost index funds:
https://www.youtube.com/watch?v=zpKi4_IJvlY
Fidelity Annuity funds with performance data.
http://fundresearch.fidelity.com/annuities/category-performance-annual-total-returns-quarterly/FPRAI?refann=005

Other resources

Most subscription services offer research on ETFs. IBD has a strategy dedicated to ETFs and so does AAII to name a couple.

Seeking Alpha has extensive resources for ETF including an ETF screener and investing ideas. So is ETFdb.

Not all ETFs are created equal
Check their performances and their expenses.

When to use or not to use ETFs
I prefer sector mutual funds in some industries, as they have many bad stocks such as drug industry, banks, miners and insurers. Most mutual funds cannot time the market.

When you believe a sector is heading up (or contra ETF for heading down), but you do not have time to do research on specific stocks, buy an ETF for the sector; it is same for the market.

Half ETF
Taking out half of the stocks that score below the average in an index ETF could beat the same full ETF itself. I call it HETF (half the ETF). You heard it here first.

To illustrate, sort the expected P/E (not including stocks with negative earnings) in ascending order and only include the stocks on the first half. Add more fundamental metrics. It will take a few minutes.

Disadvantages of ETFs
- When you have two stocks in a sector ETF one good one and one bad one, the ETF treats them the same. Stock pickers would buy the one that has a better appreciation potential.
- Sometimes the return could be misleading due to stock rotation. To illustrate this, on August 29, 2012, SHLD was replaced by LYB in a sector fund. SHLD was down by 4% and LYB was up by 4% primarily due to the switch. Unless you sell and buy at the right time (which is impossible), your return would not match the ETF's returns due to the replacement.
- Ensure the performance matches the corresponding index; it is hard due to excluding dividends.

Advantages of ETFs
- We have demonstrated that you can beat the market by using market timing. Between 2000 and Nov., 2013, you only exit and reenter the market 3 times and the result is astonishing.

- It is easy to rotate a sector vs. buying/selling all of the stocks in this sector. Rotating a sector is the same as trading a stock.
- The risk is spread out, and your portfolio is diversified especially for a market ETF or buying three or more ETFs in different sectors.
- Periodically the bad stocks in most funds are replaced by better stocks.
- Eliminate the time in researching stocks.

Leveraged ETFs
I do not recommend them. Some are 2x, 3x and even higher. They're too risky for beginners. However, when you are very sure or your tested strategy has very low drawdown, you may want to use them to improve performance. Most leveraged ETFs and contra ETFs have higher fees.

My basic ETF tables
I include some contra ETFs, mutual funds and Fidelity's annuity. Some of these may be interesting to you. Most Vanguard's ETFs have lower fees.

ETFs and funds come and go. Some ideas and classifications are my own interpretation. Refer to ETFdb for updated information. Not responsible for any error. Check out the ETF or fund before you take any action.

I prefer VFINX over SPY for the lower fees; both simulate the S&P500 index. The stocks in the ETF can be either equally weighed or weighed by market caps. The latter is more like using momentum strategy, as the rising stocks usually have larger market caps. The index usually kicks out some poor-performing stocks and replaced them with better stocks. These ETFs are suited for long-term investing without constant reviews.

Table by market cap:

Category	ETF	Mutual Funds	Fidelity's Annuity	Contra ETF	Alternate
Size:					
Large Cap	DIA			DOG	
	SPY			SH	VFINX FXAIX VOO
	QQQ			PSQ	FNCMX
	RYH				
Blend	IWD	BEQGX			
Growth	SPYG	FBGRX			FSPGX
Value	SPYV	DOGGX			FLCOX
Dividend	NOBL	FRDPX			
	VYM				
Mid Cap			FNBSC	MYY	

Blend	MDY	VSEQX			
Growth		STDIX			
		BPTRX			
Value		FSMVX			
Small Cap			FPRGC	SBB	FSSNX
Blend	IWM	HDPSX			
Growth		PRDSX			FECGX
Value		SKSEX			FISVX
Micro	IWC				
Multi					
Blend		VDEOX			
Growth		VHCOX			
Value		TCLCX			
Total					FSKAX VTI
Bond					
Long Term (20)	VLV	BTTTX		TBF	
Mid Term (7 – 10)	VCIT	FSTGX			
Short Term (1 – 3 yrs.)	VCSH	THOPX			
Total	BOND	PONDX			
Corp Invest Grade	VCIT	NTHEX			
High Yield (junk)	PHB	SPHIX			
Muni	MUB	Check state			
Special situation					
Buy back	PKW				

Table by sectors:

Sector	ETF	Mutual Funds	Fidelity's Annuity
Banking[1]		FSRBK	
Regional	IAT		
Bio Tech	IBB	FBIOX	
	XBI	Large	
Consumer Dis.	XLY	FSCPX	FVHAC
Consumer Staple	XLP	FDFAX	FCSAC

Finance	KIE	FIDSX	FONNC
	IYF		
Energy	XLE	FSENX	FJLLC
Energy Service		FSESX	
Gold	GLD	FSAGX	BAR
Gold Miner	GDX	VGPMX	
Health Care	IYH	FSPHX	FPDRC
	VHT	VGHCX	
House Builder	ITB	FSHOX	
	ITB	Perform	
Industrial	IYJ	FCYIX	FBALC
Material	VAW	FSDPX	GSG
	IYM		
Oil	USO		
Oil Service	OIH	FSESX	
Oil Exploration	XOP		
Real Estate	VNQ	FRIFX	FFWLC
REIT	VNQ		
Retail	RTH	FSRPX	
	XRT		
Regional bank	KRE	FSRBX	
Semi Conduct	SMH		
Software	XSW	FSCSX	
	IGV		
Technology	XLK	FSPTX	FYENC
	FDN	FBSOX	
		ROGSX	
Telecomm.	VOX	FSTCX	FVTAC
Transport	XTN		
	IYT		
Utilities	XLU	FSUTX	FKMSC
Wireless		FWRLX	

Footnote. [1] Also check Finance.

Table by countries outside the USA:

Country	ETF	Mutual Funds	Fidelity's Annuity	Alternate
Australia	EWA			
Brazil	EWZ			
Canada	EWC	FICDX		
China	FXI	FHKCX		
EAFE	EFA			
Emerging	VWO	FEMEX	FEMAC	FPADX
Europe	VGK	FIEUX		
Global	KXI	PGVFX		
Greece	GREK			
India	INDY	MINDX		
Indonesia	EIDO			
Latin America	ILF	FLATX		
Nordic		FNORX		
Hong Kong	EWH			
Japan	EWJ	FJPNX		
S. Africa	EZA			
S. Korea	EWY	MAKOX		
Singapore	EWS			
Taiwan	EWT			
	TUR			
United Kingdom	EWU			
Foreign:				
Combination				
Intern. Div.	IDV			FTIHX
Small Cap	SCZ			
Value	EFV			
Europe	VGK			

#Filler: Honey, my book can play music.

https://www.youtube.com/watch?v=HxGT5z6d-GA&list=PLMZa6mP7jZ2b1otqG4tfbgZpLEdh6YiNF

It may cut down commercials by casting it to TV.

Book 5: Trading Stocks

This section will answer some of the questions with regard to trading stocks. They are but not limited to:

- The fair price of your trade.
- Protect your profits.
- Make extra money with covered calls.
- Diversify your portfolio.
- Bonds.
- Taxes.
- Trading plan.
- Brokers.

The following link from Charles Schwab offers a lot of insightful articles on this topic.
http://seekingalpha.com/author/charles-schwab/articles#regular_articles

1 Chronology of a trade

This is a summary in the life of a trade as described throughout this book. In a sentence, do your due diligence (same as do your homework). It is a general summary. Modify the plan to fit your personal requirements and risk tolerance.

- Is the market favorable to buy stocks?
    - Market timing. Early Recovery, a phase of the market cycle defined by me, is the best time to invest.
    - Even in a bear market, there are valued stocks to buy but the chance is slim for appreciation.

- ETFs - If you trade ETFs only, skip the next step.
    - Know the sectors to avoid unless you are knowledgeable in the specific sectors.
    - Sector/Industry[1] risk:
        - Rank sector (many subscription services have a current rank for the sector/industry). Alternatively, check out the recent performance of the ETF for that sector.
        - Sector metrics (e.g., average for debt/equity, average P/E...).
        - Sector outlook.

- Screen stocks to buy
    - Use screens and strategies that were successful recently.
- Analyze Stocks.
    - Scoring a stock.
    - Intangible analysis.
    - Qualitative analysis.
    - Technical analysis.
- Buy a stock.
- Sell most stocks when the market is going to plunge.
- Sell a stock when the fundamentals deteriorate or objectives are met.

[1] Companies are categorized into sectors and sectors are further sub divided into industries. For example, bank is a sector and regional bank is an industry.

Filler: Consumer or stock holder
The more you bash the airlines, the more profit the airlines make.

How? The less service they give, the more profits they get and so are their stock prices. However, do not go to the extreme. Do you want to be a consumer or an investor?

2 Order prices

Market orders
It is simply trading the stock at the prevailing market price. Place market orders to buy only when the stock is moving up. Many winners never take a breather on their way up. Trade prices can easily be manipulated on stocks with low trading volumes. To reduce being manipulated, do not place market orders after hours.

Consider bid and ask. A 'bid' is the price a potential buyer would like to buy while the 'ask' is a potential seller would like to sell. Your market price is usually the worst price in either case, but it is a guarantee that you would trade the stock. A large spread would mean that it would take a longer time to use a limit order and/or the trade volume of the stock is small. A liquid stock usually have a spread of one penny or two.

In my momentum portfolio on 11/2013, I placed a sell price for GERN far higher than the market price. Surprisingly I sold it for this price making an annualized return of 1,176% for holding it for 21 days. When there are few or no other sellers for the stock, the market price would be the price you set. If I cannot sell it in the next 9 days (30 days is my holding period for momentum stocks), I would set it lower. Update: One year later, GERN lost 29%.

Sensible discounts
I prefer to buy the stock at the price closest to the last trade price (to most it is the market price) via a limit order. I seldom lose buying these orders. Sometimes I use the day's lowest price to buy (or the highest to sell) plus a penny (or minus a penny for sell prices to sell).

My other purchase strategy is using 0.15% or 0.25% less than the current prices for stocks I really want. For some promising stocks, I buy them at almost the market price and then place another order on the same stock at 0.5% less than the last traded price (and sometimes 2% depending on the current market trend).

We all want to buy less and sell at higher prices. However, if the trade price is too far away from the current market price (such as 5% from the market price), these trades may never be executed. I have had a long list of buy orders that were not executed and turned out to be big gainers. Learn from my bad experiences.

Use a good discount (such as 10% from the market price) if you believe the market, the sector or the stock will dip by 10%. After you bought the stock, you place a sell order 10% more than the price you paid for it hoping the stock will return to the original price and you pocket 10%. Wishful thinking! However, it has happened to me several times primarily due to temporary market dips.

It works when there is a correction and/or the stock is very volatile. It is usually within the 5% range to take advantage of these situations, not the 10% as described. For a 10% plunge, it usually is due to some serious problem of the company surfacing. One common reason is not meeting its earnings expectation and in this case it usually continues its downward trend.

Larger discounts on a falling market
During a falling market (or a mild correction), 3% less than the current prices for buy orders may be fine for some stocks (use 5% for volatile stocks). To illustrate, I placed about 10 of these orders over the last two months during a market dip. Most of the orders were filled. When the market is plunging, do not buy any stock.

Caterpillar and Cisco were some of my buys at these discounts. They were in my watch list to buy. Initially these shares often fall even lower as the trend was downward. As of 12/18/12, CAT earned me from 3% and 14% (bought in 6/12 and 7/12) and CSCO bought in 7/14/12 returned about 34%. My original objective: Buy deeply-valued stocks, wait and sell them when the economy returns.

When you predict the market will dip by 5%, set your buy orders accordingly. Again, predictions are just educated guesses. From my experience, they work most of the time but not all of the time.

On the day of the earnings announcement, the fluctuation of the stock is usually high. Check any change in the earnings estimate before the announcement and act accordingly. Zacks is supposed to be a useful tool to predict earnings estimates. Do not leave orders during the earnings announcement dates, which can be found in Finviz. When the earning turns out to be good, the stock price surges and your order will not be executed. When the earnings are bad, the stock price will plunge usually and you most likely over-payed.

Option expiration dates usually cause more volatility. Retail investors do not have to be concerned except you may use wider stops. In theory, dividend days have little effect on the stock price as it will be lowered by the dividend amount.

High volume of a stock could mean opportunity High volume usually increases the stock price volatility. If the volatility of a stock increases substantially (such as doubling its average daily volume), there could be important news on the company, recommendation changes from a major analyst or trading by the institutional investors. It usually takes the institutional investors a week to trade a stock with their sizable positions.

Many times it is started by the insiders who know about the breaking news of a stock before it is publicized. Some investment services / sites specialize in identifying the increasing volumes on these stocks.

Because day traders do not want to leave any open positions overnight, higher volatility occurs at the end of the day. It is the same on the day (usually on Friday) when the options are expiring.

Monitor your trade prices
You cannot tell whether you are paying a fair price without keeping a record. To illustrate, you're paying 1% less than the market prices in buying stocks. You may have missed buying some winners. If the 1% you saved is smaller than the appreciation of the stocks you would have bought at market prices, then you should adjust the buy prices to 0.5% less than the market price and monitor again.

Market trend makes a difference too. When the market is trending up, buying any stock would most likely be profitable and usually the purchase orders with higher discounts will not be executed.

Follow the same logic on sell orders. Need to have at least 25 stock purchases (and potential purchases) to make the conclusion meaningful. If you do not trade a lot, you will not have enough data to verify. As described, I prefer not to place an order during the earnings announcement dates which can be found in Finviz.com. If you cannot buy the stock, consider to use market order the next day. With most brokers offer no commission trades, the "All or none" option is not valid.

Good prospects When you find gems especially those stocks that are followed by analysts, buy them at market prices and consider doubling the bet if you are really sure you have a winner. From my super stock screens, I spotted NHTC. I placed several bets and one market order. All of them were NOT executed except with the market order. At the end of the day NHTC is up 18% and my executed order is up 14%. I did not have the best buy but made a good profit. NHTC was on its way to a huge appreciation and I sold it too early. I have earned not to sell a winner and protect the profit with a stop.

Lower the buy for risky stocks (if the beta from Finviz is greater than 1 for example) even if they have good fundamentals.

Quality over quantity

If your time is limited, spend all the time on researching one stock one at a time. However, you need to own at least 3 stocks (more stocks for a large portfolio) for your diversification purposes.

Double your normal purchase position on stocks that look great after the research. For risky stocks that look good, you may want to halve your normal purchase position to cut down on the risk. If you are less risk tolerant, do not buy risky stocks at all. My results are not conclusive on risky stocks but I do get a good sleep.

A recent example

Recently I sold EA with $1 more than my order price but $2 less than the current price of the day, which was the earnings announcement day. I do recommend not placing orders right before the earnings announcement day for the stock. If the earnings are good, you do not get all the profit as in this real example; my broker did get me $1 more. If the earnings are bad, you will not sell it any way. It is the same for buying stocks.

Afterthoughts

- Besides luck, the smart investor never sells at the peak but usually within 10% of the peak. No one can predict the peaks consistently.
- My personal experiences. I have to use market orders for stocks are heading up. Sometimes I have two buy orders for the same stock, one has a far better price. Most likely I can get the buy orders executed by placing one cent less than the lowest price. When the market is heading down, I place buy orders more favorable to me.
- I made mistakes like most of you. One time my buy price was higher than the last price executed. Luckily my broker adjusted it to the right price but I may not be that lucky next time. Several times I switched the buy price and sell price by mistake. One time it was due to my boss coming by that forced me to enter my order hastily. Try to avoid the first hour of a trade session.

- Some experts do not suggest their clients to buy stocks on the way down. With respect, I offer opposing arguments.
    - It is fine to buy them on the way down, if you have the conviction that the company or the economy will recover.
    - No one knows where the bottom is, but averaging down could be beneficial if the company or the economy can recover. Check why its stock price is falling and whether the company can fix its problems. Some major problems are only temporary or easy to fix.
    - Most of my big profits are made by buying close to the bottom prices on stocks that have a good potential to recover.
    - Many value stocks are on sale when the market dips. The most favorable time is in the Early Recovery, a phase in the market cycle defined by me.
    - Most experts agree that: The best time to buy is when there is blood in the street. It is demonstrated by the year 2003 and 2009.
    - Contrarians never follow the herd, but you need to have a good reason to be contrary. I recommended Apple in 2013 when every institutional investor was dumping Apple.
    - Stocks are manipulated via selling shorts. When the shares of a stock to short (like over 30% of shorts) are running out, there is a good chance for a short squeeze. Ensure the company being shorted heavily is not heading into bankruptcy.
- Make good money when you are right only 45% of the time by: 1. Limit your losses via stops and 2. Place higher stakes on stocks with higher appreciation potential.
- Some make money on earnings announcement (found in Finviz.com). Earnings would amplify the stock price by at least 5%. Once in a while, there are exceptions. In the last quarter of 2015, Disney posted great results, but the stock dropped. It could be that the market even expected better results or the market is not rational. I believe the later in this case.
- Many foreign stocks that are listed in U.S. exchanges have extra hefty fees.
- As of 5/2021, the following stocks have been appreciated shortly but their buy orders have not been executed: FL (by 25%), MTZ (31%), RBNC (17%), ANIP (30%), METC (34%), etc. To avoid this from recurring, I would increase the buy prices and even use market orders if necessary.

Links
Selling short:
http://en.wikipedia.org/wiki/Short_%28finance%29
Short squeeze:
http://en.wikipedia.org/wiki/Short_squeeze
Fidelity Video: Stop Loss.
https://www.fidelity.com/learning-center/trading/trailing-stops-video
https://www.youtube.com/watch?v=l7EHWyOrfu4

3   Stop loss & flash crash

You can limit your stock losses with stops. When the stock price falls into the stop you specified, it will trigger a sell order at the market price. A stop-limit order is similar to stop order except it triggers a sell order with a price you specified; hence the sell order may not be executed. There are some incidents where you do not always want to use a stop loss.

- Flash crash (May 6, 2010 and August 2015).
  It would turn your stops into market orders that could be substantially lower than your stop prices. Some brokers offer stop limits, but they do not guarantee the orders will be executed.

  The better way is a "mental stop" (my term). You do not place a stop order but place a market order to sell when your stock falls below a predefined price. During flash crashes, you do not want to place the market orders to sell but place orders to buy from your watch list.

  I bought some stocks at more than 10% discount during the flash crash (actually I could buy them even at better discounts) and within a week most had returned to the prices as before the flash crash.

  Placing buy orders with huge discounts to the market prices works better for volatile stocks. You should cancel the unexecuted trades before the weekends / holidays and reenter them afterwards to avoid unexpected events that may affect the stock prices.

  Avoid trading drug and biotech companies with huge differences to the market prices. High tech is a good sector for this purpose and fluctuating 10% in this sector is more of a norm than an exception. Buying an ETF at 5% discount is a better bet than buying specific stocks from my experience.

- My experience with 911.
  I sold many stocks due to stop orders during 911. The market came back in the next three days and I missed the recovery from the stocks that were sold and did not buy back them in time.

- If your stocks are rising, you need to adjust the stop loss prices accordingly. To illustrate- in maintaining a 10% stop loss, your stop is at 90 when the current price is 100. When the stock price rises to 200, it should be adjusted to $180 (10% less than the current price). It is also called a trailing stop. Need to review these rising stocks, and change the stop price periodically (one week to one month depending on how volatile the stock is).

Most brokers allow you to enter most trades "Good till Cancelled". Even for that there is an expiration date such as 6 months for Fidelity. Fidelity's trades for Short Sell expire by the end of the trade session. Check your broker's current policy.

- Risky markets.
  When the market is risky, you may want to use a stop loss. To prevent another flash crash, you may want to use a 'mental' market order. It is not perfect, as it requires constant watching of the market.

  There are many investing services and sites that give you the 'right' prices for a stop loss. Basically it depends on how volatile the specific stocks are. The chartists will tell you under normal conditions stocks are trading between the resistance line and the support line. Use the stop loss just below the resistance line to avoid the stop order from being executed due to the volatility of the stock.

  For simplicity as I have too many stocks in my portfolio, I use a percent. In the old days, it was recommended 8% or so below the prices you paid. In today's volatile market, I recommend 12%.

- Risky stocks.
  A stop loss is the only way that you can limit your loss for a big drop (such as 25%). Affimax lost 85% of its stock value in one day with the news that three of its patients died.

- Low-volume stocks.
  The market order could drive the prices right down as there are few buyers in low-volume stocks. If there is only one buyer, he will buy with the best price for him (or the worst price to the seller). It could be easily **manipulated** especially after the trading hours. For example, the manipulator could buy the stock at a low price to trigger the stop order. I learn it the hard way. I would use mental stops: When I see the stock is below a specified value, I would sell it via a market price.

  Unless I have good reasons, I would skip the low-volume stocks. I define low-volume: If my buy amount is higher than 1% of the average daily amount (= average daily volume * stock price).

- Beta.
  Stocks may be more volatile than the market. Beta is used to measure its volatility. The market can be measured by the S&P 500 index. If the beta of a stock is 1, its volatility is the same as the market. If it is 1.2, it is 20% more volatile.

  Set a lower stop loss for volatile stocks to prevent stocks from selling due to regular fluctuations.

What should be the stop price?

Basically, you do not want to sell the stock via a stop order during the regular fluctuations. If it happens (sometimes stops do not work as expected), buy the stock back ensuring it is not a wash sale in taxable accounts.

Many web sites have suggestions of the stop price. Usually Finviz and Fidelity have the resistance line in the charts. You select the order price slightly below the resistance line.

For simplicity, select 12% less than your purchase price (more or less depending on the market volatility). For example, the purchase price is $100, use the stop price $88 (=100 – 12). Also, change the stop price even lower if the stock is volatile according to its beta (available in Finviz).

If your stock rises, you want to adjust the stop price higher and it should be based on the current price (not your purchase price). In this case, I would review it more often (say a month). It is similar to the trailing stop. Most brokers provide you a percent or a stop price. Personally I use 15% and 20% for volatile stocks. You need to review it periodically as many orders could expire as the period may be determined by your broker.

Links
https://www.investopedia.com/ask/answers/06/stoplossorderdetails.asp
https://www.investopedia.com/terms/t/trailingstop.asp

4   Tax avoidance

Tax avoidance is a good way to save some money legally. Tax laws change all the time. Check Wikipedia on current investment taxes. Consult your tax lawyer as my knowledge in taxes is limited, and the tax laws are always changing.

In general for Federal returns on your taxable accounts (as opposed to IRA, Roth IRA, IRA-Rollover and 401K), you have to pay taxes on dividends either at the ordinary income rate or at a qualified rate which is usually lower. If the stock that was held longer than a year, you pay long-term capital tax (max. 20% as of 2020). The short-term capital tax rate at the ordinary income rate is up to 37% as of 2020. In addition, you may have to pay state and local taxes. Currently, you can offset $3,000 or up to your total losses from your regular income.

Do not implement what I did as tax laws change frequently and every one's situation is different. Here is what I did and I hope it will be applicable to you.

- Sold the most profitable stocks that I held more than a year in taxable accounts in 2021 to qualify for long-term capital gains. Usually they have more favorable tax treatments than the short-term capital gains, which are treated as ordinary income. I bought some back. I maintained a 15% tax bracket, so the tax bill from Uncle Sam is virtually 0 (not exactly due to more tax on social security and Medicare as a result of the trades). I still had to pay state tax. As a retiree, I can control my income

- Converted part of my Rollover IRA to Roth in 2012 and 2013. I paid taxes today. However, the Roth conversion gives me tax-free appreciation for the future trades in this account and it will lower taxes and my minimum withdrawal requirement in the future. Check whether it is still available.

- The taxes from dividends in the retirement accounts are deferred but eventually they will be treated as regular income when they are withdrawn. Very few people have higher income during their retirement. If you are the lucky few due to the successful investing in your retirement accounts, you may end up with a higher tax bracket during your retirement, particularly when you are forced to withdraw at age 70 ½.

- Gifted some appreciated stocks to my children. The current price of the gifted stock is used in calculating the total cost allowed, not the price you paid for them. The long-term capital gains may be waived for adult children with incomes below a specified level. I prefer the value stocks that have potential for long-term appreciation. It is good for them and not good for Uncle Sam. You can gift up to $15,000 (in 2021) for each spouse to each child without paying any Federal tax. For a family of four, you and your spouse can gift up to $60,000 (= 15,000 * 4) a year. It is a long time before your children or grandchildren withdraw, it is better to use an ETF that stimulates the market such as SPY. Also consider the loop back period for gifts. Check out this link. https://www.irs.gov/businesses/small-businesses-self-employed/frequently-asked-questions-on-gift-taxes

The cost basis of the transferred stock is quite complicated. Check out the current tax law. The cost basis of the appreciated stocks is carried to the receiver, so it would lower your capital taxes as most of us are in higher tax brackets than our children.

From my experience, the cost basis of the depreciated stocks after the transfer is the market price on the transfer day as of 2016. I do not understand it enough to comment but just to tell you what I have experienced. I tried to offset my son's unexpected short-term capital gain by transferring a losing stock and that did not work.

- My lawyer set up trusts for me including my house. They will hopefully avoid probate. From the current tax law (as of 2016), the cost basis of your stocks will be stepped up or down to the stock prices on that day you pass away. Ask your heirs to keep a business paper for the stock prices or tell your brokers to adjust the cost basis on the day you pass away. Of course, you have to tell your heirs now to take care of these tasks. Again, ask your tax lawyer for details.

  Make sure you specify the beneficiaries in your and your spouse's accounts to avoid probate. Check your local state laws. Some states take more than a year to finish the probate process for a house. As of 2014, my state (Mass.) has an exemption of 1 million, not portable to your spouse, and they calculate the entire estate when it exceeds the exemption. There is no estate tax if my estate is a million dollars. I have to pay a rate on 1,000,001 if it just exceeds it by one dollar. That's why we should move 20 miles north to New Hampshire.

  I estimate that it takes about three years for the average estate to be distributed. You want to cut down the duration by having a will to start with, so you do not want to pay extra for your lawyer.

- At age 70 ½ (as of 2021), you are required to withdraw them in a schedule and it could put you in a higher tax bracket. Roth withdrawal is not counted in the mandatory withdrawal for a person's lifetime. Check the current tax laws.
- Roth IRAs, if qualified, could be the best deal for most. However, you have to use after-tax money to fund your Roth IRA.
- I simulate my next year via my tax preparation software and adjust my income accordingly.
- Most oil partnerships and many MLPs require you to file special tax forms for non-retirement accounts in 2017. I avoided most of them as my time is limited. Some ETFs require you to file the complicated K-1 (vs 1099) in your tax return. You can find this requirement in ETFdb.com. You can avoid them

by not buying these ETFs, or buy them in my non-taxable accounts. Usually the taxes on these dividends are lowered as they are treated as the return of investment after depreciation.
- There is a $500,000 exemption from the profits of selling your house with some restrictions.

- Harvest the tax loss for future use and take the $3,000 offset to your income. My state does not allow me to write off the $3,000. Hence, my short-term loss for the future is $3,000 more for my state than the Federal.

- Avoid wash sales in your taxable accounts
  http://en.wikipedia.org/wiki/Wash_sale

  You cannot claim the loss for the year if you buy back the stock within 30 days. Before I buy, I check whether I sold this loser in the last 30 days. Before I sell a loser, I check whether I bought it in the last 30 days.

  I placed one order to sell a loser at a higher price and another one to buy it back at a lower price. When there is a big swing in price for that stock, both orders were executed within 30 days. I cannot claim the loss of the sold stock for that year. However, the loss can be adjusted to the cost basis of the newly-acquired stock as of 2013.

  There are many ways to avoid it. Try not to buy it back within 30 days (check the current regulation) and this is the best way. IRS has more restrictions and it is better not to push it to the limit. Buy a similar stock in the same sector. Buy it in your children's account. Again, check the current tax laws.
  - I bought my annuity trying to save taxes after all retirement accounts had been fully funded. So far, it turns out my tax rate is higher after retirement. I do not recommend most annuities due to the fees. Most annuities have high commission fees and that is why most financial advisors want to sell them to you.

Afterthoughts

- Tax audit signs.
  http://money.cnn.com/gallery/pf/taxes/2014/03/14/tax-audit/index.html?iid=HP_LN
  Your business would be treated as a hobby if you do not have a profit in three out of the last five years. Day traders and businesses can deduct all the trading expenses. Some form an investing company in some Caribbean island to avoid paying taxes. Again check the current tax laws.
- As of 2013, the dividend tax is at 20% max. Do not believe it is no tax in tax-deferred accounts. When you withdraw, it will be treated as a regular income and it can be as high as almost 40% (as of 2013). Your dividend tax rate depends on your income.

- When you trade 5 times or more a week, investigate whether you're eligible to trade as a business by the current tax rule. A business allows its owner to deduct business expenses.
- Fidelity: Investment tax.
  https://www.fidelity.com/learning-center/mutual-funds/tax-implications-bond-funds

  ETF Taxes on Foreign Stocks: http://seekingalpha.com/article/2491465-foreign-withholding-taxes-in-international-equity-etfs

Links

Tax Avoidance:
http://en.wikipedia.org/wiki/Tax_avoidance
Tax Law: http://en.wikipedia.org/wiki/Income_tax_%28U.S.%29
Without paying (gift tax):
http://en.wikipedia.org/wiki/Gift_tax_in_the_United_States#Gift_tax_exemptions
http://www.irs.gov/Businesses/Small-Businesses-&-Self-Employed/What%27s-New---Estate-and-Gift-Tax
AMT: http://en.wikipedia.org/wiki/Alternative_minimum_tax
Estate planning fun. http://tonyp4idea.blogspot.com/2014/08/estate-planning-101-for-me.html
Taxes on stocks: https://www.youtube.com/watch?v=EKYMbsjUUtE
Tax avoidance: https://www.youtube.com/watch?v=tXou5pM7zh0
Capital gain: https://www.youtube.com/watch?v=ezPs4ibFsNU&t=2678s

5   Brokers

Protect the security of your financial transactions. Do not hit any web link that you do not know including those 'good' deals – your greed could cause you to lose millions! I use my Chrome for these transactions and I do not access my e-mails via this Chrome. A two-step log in (if available) should be useful. The broker sends you a temporary log-in password to your mobile phone. Install anti-virus software such as Norton and Malwarebytes. Do not use the mobile phone for trading stocks and stay away from 'free Wi-Fi' networks. Besides your broker account, tax info, bank accounts and credit card are the next important things that you need to protect.

Today most brokers are discount brokers, and many are commission-free. Choose one to start with and two should be the maximum.

The following is for illustration purposes only as I should not recommend any broker. Fidelity offers a lot of research free and commission-free trades (similar to Charles Schwab), extensive mutual funds and bank/credit card services. Interactive Broker has a low margin rate (vs. Fidelity's 9% or so today) and low commissions on some transactions. Many others have their own advantages. If you only need one broker, select the one based on your requirements.

Today many brokers offer many trading options that were not available 15 years ago such as trading a stock with specific condition(s) and canceling an order based on certain condition(s). For example, you can have a stop order and a limited sell order on the same stock.

Full-service brokers offer some services most discount brokers do not offer. One offers buying IPO stocks and selling them automatically at the end of the day. This strategy had been doing well except in 2015. Do not believe you can pay someone to manage your portfolio and you're all set. There have been cases of portfolio churning to generate income for the broker.

There are many magazine articles comparing brokers. I do not really care whether the order is executed in 1 or 5 micro seconds. However, I do find some orders have been traded better by one broker over another. What do you mean 'by traded better' you may ask? The followings are examples. I cannot prove whether they are true or not but to me, it seems to be true.

- I have identical buy orders placed with two brokers. Consistently one broker gets them executed more often than the other broker.
- One broker often gives me better prices than the other. For example, my sell price was $10, and many times I got more than $10 such as $10.02.
- One broker has more reversed orders than the other. For example, I was informed my order was executed but they told me it had been reversed on the second day.
- One consistently charged extra fees. I understand it is tough to make the paper-thin commissions today.
- ADR fees. Some are quite hefty. I avoid many foreign stocks. Some charge more for the gains especially France. At one time, most ADR stocks did well, but not anymore as the US stocks have been doing well (as of 2/2017). The ADR fees are charged by your broker or bank. The following is from a Kiplinger's article.

"ADRs, which represent shares of ownership in a foreign company, trade in the U.S. in dollars. Some ADRs come with a contractual provision that allows the broker, in this case TD Ameritrade, to levy "depositary services fees."

The charges, commonly 2 cents per share, are intended to cover the cost of coordinating overseas investments. For ADRs that include this provision, the broker can levy the charge at any time, but no more than once a year.

Margin
Margin should not be used extensively. It is expensive and most brokers try every trick to squeeze profits from all transactions to subsidize their low-commission incomes. Usually you can borrow up to 40% of your current position and the margin rates vary among brokers. Check out your broker's margin rate. In general, margin is not allowed in your retirement accounts. You may need to file an application for margin. Your brokers ensure you meet specific requirements to lower their risk such as your income.

Many lost a lot during the last two market plunges. However, many including myself made a killing in 2003 and 2009 using margin. I use it for the following reasons. For convenience in placing buy orders that exceed my cash position in my taxable accounts.

I pay back my outstanding margin loan from my home equity loan (check the current tax law) as it is far, far lower than my broker's margin interest rate.

Tips and tricks
- Many brokers' promotions offers you cash and/or free trades (no longer needed as many brokers offer commission-free trades) if you deposit a specific amount in your account. Without commission cost, you do not need to round up to a lot size (100 shares in most cases) nor specify "All or None". Check the details of the offers. Some give you free trades only up to 60 days while others offer up to two years. If your broker cancels your 'completed' orders or never gives you trade prices better than the ones you enter, it is time to change broker.
- Some brokers restrict withdrawal in a specific time frame such as one year or during the period of the free commission. After that, you can move it to another broker that gives you similar deals. In most cases, the offer is per social security number or per person. A bad execution of a trade is not worth the free commission and/or any goodies.
- If you need margin a lot such as shorting stocks, check out the margin rates from different brokers.
- Most brokers offer basic trading lessons and market reviews. Most are well-written.
- Most brokers offer stock evaluation. Some are really good with proven records. Take advantage of it.
- Many brokers offer two-phase logon for better security. Many send you a security code to your mobile phone or your email account. Then you enter the code.
- Ignore filling out the forms for group lawsuits unless your stock holding is large. I received $20 for spending at least 2 hours to find my statement.
- Some brokers offer free commissions for specific ETFs. For sector rotation trades, it could add up to a lot of savings. Today it is not relevant to most brokers as they are already commission-free. So is the "All but none" option during entering a trade.
- Some brokers may require you to confirm if you want to trade using margin, options, penny stocks, risky stocks and after-hour trading.
- My broker calculates my performance returns and compares them to the indexes. It is handy.
- Interactive Broker has low margin rate. Here is a comparison of 3 major brokers. https://www.youtube.com/watch?v=rAewPVEjeLM.

6   Money Market, CDs & Bonds

I have sold many stocks to prepare for a market crash. I'm a very conservative investor. Do not follow my actions exactly as everyone's situation is different. Adjust your actions according to your risk tolerance.

As of 2019, the market was still making new highs. From my own **predictions**, today may be similar to 2007, the peaking phase of the last market cycle (termed as melt up).

I had too much cash and most of it was in money market funds in my brokers' accounts. Many of my one-year CDs paid about 1.5%. After inflation and taxes, it is a loss, but it is far better than virtually nothing from the money market funds. Our financial system punishes us for not taking risk. However, at the market peaks, we need to play defensively with conservative investments such as CDs.

The holding periods of my CDs depend on when I need the cash to buy contra ETFs such as SH during a predicted market plunge. I don't predict the market will crash in 3 months. Even if it would, I should have enough cash then within a short period of time.

Another consideration is the interest rate hikes. I predict that there would be 0.5% increase in 6 months. Hence, all the new CDs in 6 months will have 0.5% increase in interest with my theory.

We can "ladder" the CDs letting them mature in different months. For example, we can have one CD maturing in 3 months and another one in 12 months. When the first CD matures, we renew it for another 3 months. In this method, we always have cash in 3 months and one CD has a higher interest rate. The more the CDs you have, the better the distribution will be.

Ensure that the FDIC limit of $250,000 is per bank, NOT per account. Some CDs from foreign banks which are also insured by the FDIC offer higher interest rates such as the Bank of China as of this writing. Many brokers sell CDs in units and one unit represents $1,000.

Some states offer special favorable treatment for taxing interest for CDs from local banks. Being a Mass. resident, I prefer local banks. However, the CDs from my brokers make it easy to trade and select the better rates. In one case, my bank offered a special CD deal of 1.55% for 14 months. It saved me about $200 for 2 trips to go to the bank (vs. doing it on-line).

Do not select CDs that are callable. It means the banks have the right to cancel the deal for their advantage. It is no longer a popular feature – you can cheat folks sometimes, but not all the time. Try to select the CDs having the settlement date closest to today's date. Otherwise, you do not get interest on the extra days.

For the last 5 years, SPY is returning 15% and beats the 1.3% CDs by a good margin. Today buying CDs is an insurance bet. When the market crashes, it usually is fast and deep.

SPY, simulating S&P 500, is market cap weighted. It means Apple has a far larger share than the other 499 stocks. The top five stocks are the rocket stocks to me. It would be less risky if the 500 stocks are evenly weighted.

Other safe investment besides CDs

You may also consider bond funds and/or bond ETFs. They have higher dividends but most likely they are more risky. Today I do not consider long-term bonds. Their performances are inversely proportional to the interest rate. I predict there will be interest hikes. Short-term (less than two years for me) bonds are fine.

Compare the performance of the bond funds. Most make a mistake by comparing the current performance. You should compare their performances during market peaks such as in 2007 and 1999.

The two ETFs I consider are HYG and JNK. Their annualized returns are compounded. SPY is the bench mark I use. Check out their past performances.

In 2008, the market crashed. It was a bad year for bond funds and ETFs. Based on this, I would sell them when the market crashes. However, in 2009 both recovered from the previous losses quite nicely.

	2007	2008	2009
HYG	3%	-18%	29%
JNK	Not avail.	-25%	38%
SPY	5%	-37%	26%

7   Covered calls

For basic descriptions on a covered call from Wikipedia, click here or enter (http://en.wikipedia.org/wiki/Covered_call) in your browser.

It is like collecting rent from the apartment you bought. The difference is that the renter has an option to buy the apartment at a preset time and price.

The rent is quite substantial if you do good planning. To start with, you want to buy stocks that have a market to sell. Usually they are large companies with high trading volumes.

Since one contract is for 100 shares of a stock, you cannot sell a covered call on 50 shares of a stock. On the other hand, when you have 1,000 stocks, the commission of 10 contracts would be more than the cost of 1 contract depending on your broker's schedule.

It is time consuming to keep track of the covered calls but it is well worth your time and effort. If the stock price exceeds the strike price of your covered call, you may want to buy the same shares back, so you would not miss any further appreciation of this stock.

However, if it is in a taxable account and you have a loss in a forced sell, do not buy it back otherwise the tax loss is not allowed (i.e. a wash sale) for the year as of 2016. When the contract expires, you may want to start another contract on the same stock if the stock has not been sold.

Covered calls do have their disadvantages such as higher commission rates and sometimes forcing you to sell at a higher tax rate for short-term capital gains in taxable accounts. It is avoidable by using covered calls on stocks that are qualified for long-term capital gains. In addition, you need to buy them back when they increase in price beyond your strike price or lose its potential to appreciate further. Using another put could keep you from not losing any gains beyond the strike price. However, I prefer to use my time in more productive ways and this insurance is not cheap. One's opinion.

One company advertises their techniques using covered calls which could give their users 3 to 6% monthly returns. If you believe in this fantasy, you do not need this book. There is no free lunch.

My recent experience

I sold Netflix covered calls with the strike price about 2% higher and a 3% premium (from my memory) but the price shot up 12% higher in one day, so I was potentially losing 7% profit. However, it turned out to be a good experience as Netflix went downhill later (8/2012).

Normally I prefer to sell covered options for stocks with a quantity from 100 to 600 shares (i.e. 1 to 6 contracts) for the longest time (about 2-3 months). Some non-volatile and small stocks are not candidates to write covered calls on. Some stocks are not optionable. Typically high-tech stocks have a higher premium to be collected as their stock prices fluctuate more. The right stocks can generate 10% or even more a year in addition to the fluctuations of the stock prices.

In general, if I feel the market will be down for the period, I use covered calls especially for stocks holding over one year (unless I have short-term loss to offset any short-term gains) in taxable accounts. Watch out for any tax change that may affect your total return.

Recently I attended a sales pitch on a 3-day training course on a strategy for making 24% per year and it is quite possible especially with the S&P 500 returns about the same. I wish it were available to me 15 years ago. It seems to be too good to be true.

How to sell covered calls

First you need to open an account with your broker and apply to trade options including covered calls.

Check how your broker charges commissions. Ask how much they charge for one contract and 10 contracts of a stock.

The covered call is an agreement to sell the rights to the buyer of the stock at the strike price for a specific date range (a.k.a. expiration date). Typically options expire on Fridays.

You need to write covered calls on the stocks you already own. One contract is 100 shares of stocks. Check out the option chain to select the price, expiration period and the strike price. Normally, the strike price should be higher than the current market price. You may want to have an expiration date 2 weeks or longer. When the contract is expiring in a few days, the contract has little value and most likely the small 'rent' is not worth the risk and the commission.

When the covered call is sold, you receive the 'rent' immediately and any dividend during the 'rental' period.

When the option is 'called' due to a price rise above the strike price, your stock will be sold and you will have to pay the regular commission.

At this point, evaluate the stock to check whether you want to buy it back. If the stock surges, you may have to pay a higher price – thus losing the extra appreciation. In addition, you may have to pay a higher capital gains tax if it is held less than the required period for long-term capital gains in a taxable account.

Note. Notice that some stocks are not optionable and/or not practical to write options on. Most brokers charge a flat rate for the first contract (such as $7) and an incremental fee for each additional contract. Shop around as the fees vary if you write a lot of covered calls.

The best stocks for covered calls are large US companies with a large average volume. The option (a.k.a. the 'rent') pays better for volatile companies such as high-tech companies. From my rough estimates for illustration purposes, the annualized return on covered calls for AAPL is 25% and C is 12% after commission.

#Filler: Double standard
We set up our standard in everything and the entire world has to follow our standard. Shooting citizens at each other, separating children from the illegals, and police brutality are fine according to our standard.

#Filler: Rocket stocks

As of 6/2017, TSLA, AMAZ, NFLX and AAPL were all over-priced by most fundamental metrics. However, they are the darlings of institutional investors. My advice is not to do anything (not to buy and not to short them) as we cannot fight the city hall and their momentum.

Book 6: Finding Stocks

There are about 4,000 of stocks (about 30,000 if you include smaller stocks and stocks on foreign exchanges). How can you find the winners? Screening stocks can give you a manageable list of candidates worth your further evaluation.

You can use one of the simple screens that are available to you free from many web sites such as Finviz.com and the one from your broker to find a handful of stocks. The filter criteria could be "P/E < 10", "Sales Growth by 20%" or a combination. If the screens consistently find you winners, they are good.

It is more complicated than that. Otherwise there will be no poor folks. However, most screened stocks should be evaluated. Among the 50 or so screens, there is only one evergreen screen that gives consistent stocks that perform. Some screens work better than others in different phases of the market cycle and/or different market conditions such as during the end of year. You need to use different screens for different purposes. For example, stress on value parameters such as "P/E" for value stocks that have to be held for a longer time than momentum stocks.

1 Where the web sites are

- **Free and simple screen sites**

    They are described in this article or type the following
    http://stocks.about.com/od/researchtools/a/071909screenlist.htm

    o Yahoo!Finance.
       Click here or type
       http://screener.finance.yahoo.com/stocks.html

    o Finviz.
       Click here or type
       http://Finviz.com/screener.ashx

       How to scan using Finviz (YouTube).
       https://www.YouTube.com/watch?v=aQ_0FTg9Cfw

Screening using technical indicators (particularly useful for momentum stocks).
https://www.YouTube.com/watch?v=RZRP2NeSX0s

- o   Your broker.
  Fidelity's screens are more sophisticated than most.

- o   More options: Google, CNBC.com and Moringstar.com.

Here is a list.
http://stocks.about.com/od/researchtools/a/071909screenlist.htm

- **Sophisticated screens (usually not free)**

Most of them are more complicated and need time to learn. Both Vector Vest and Stock123 provide historical databases for back testing your screens. Zacks has an earnings revision database at extra cost. GuruFocus has an easy-to-use but powerful screen function.

AAII provides screened stocks from various screens in its low-priced subscription. Both AAII and Value Line take care of some specific industries, but they provide no historical database at least for regular subscriptions. AAII provides historical performance summaries of their screens included in its subscription.

Afterthoughts

Here are the links to screens provided by Marketwatch and NASDAQ.
http://www.marketwatch.com/tools/stockre...
http://www.nasdaq.com/reference/stock-sc...

How to find quality stocks.
http://seekingalpha.com/article/2381395-how-to-identify-quality-stocks-and-is-there-really-alpha-to-be-had
Swing trading: https://www.youtube.com/watch?v=cMmW12Smmt4

Filler
"Sell in May" could be a self-fulfilled prophecy. I prefer to sell on April 1 and come back on Oct. 15 to avoid the herd.

2 Finviz.com screener

You should use fundamental metrics for fundamental stocks, growth metrics for growth stocks, momentum metrics for momentum stocks, or a combination. Basically you want to keep the fundamental stocks longer so the market would realize their values.

Finviz.com provides a screening function incorporating both fundamental and technical metrics and is one of the best free sites. Bring up Finviz.com in your browser and select screener. You have 4 tabs: Descriptive, Fundamental, Technical and All. It has the following features:

- The criteria specified can be saved but the number is limited.
- The searched stocks can be saved in a portfolio (for paper trading and performance monitoring).
- Technical indicators.
- For an extra fee, you can have a historical database. This would help you to test your strategies. The historical database is quite limited for some technical parameters only.
- Some advanced technical indicators work well especially useful in momentum trading.
- Use technical patterns. My favorites are Head and Shoulder and Double Bottoms (Peaks).
- Combine fundamental metrics and technical metrics to narrow down your selection.
- Combine fundamental metrics and technical metrics to narrow down your selection.
- Add Insider Trans (> 5% for me), Short Squeeze (> 20%), etc. for specific purposes.
- [Candlesticks](#) is hard to master. You need to read a book dedicated to it.
  http://www.investopedia.com/terms/c/candlestick.asp
  https://www.youtube.com/watch?v=FsqoV1aVrUc

  https://www.youtube.com/watch?v=vQHAOcKVmA0

Finviz's screener lacks the following features:

- Stocks with prices trending up in the last several weeks (such as increasing X% in the previous week).
- Using exponential moving averages that supposedly have better predictive power than simple moving averages for momentum investing.

- Selecting ranges such as selecting all three major exchanges and market cap ranges.
- P/E for an ETF. It can be obtained from other sources such as ETFdb.com.
- When the earnings (E) is negative, you may have the wrong values for P/E and the metrics using E. For example, if you want stocks with P/E less than 20, the screener returns you stocks with negative earnings.
- Combine fundamental metrics and technical metrics to narrow down your selection.

All of these missing features can be worked around. The paid version may provide better functions.

Useful articles / YouTubes

Investopedia.
http://www.investopedia.com/university/features-of-Finviz-elite/other-chart-features.asp

How to scan using Finviz (YouTube).
https://www.YouTube.com/watch?v=aQ_0FTg9Cfw

Finviz's screener tutorial.
https://www.youtube.com/watch?v=glMtwB7OVf4
https://www.youtube.com/watch?v=tHtovnCY6uY
(Recommended)

Swing trading
https://www.youtube.com/watch?v=M8sNMhPJINU
Screening using technical indicators (YouTube).
https://www.YouTube.com/watch?v=RZRP2NeSX0s

Filler
Starbucks is being sued for too many ice cubes in the ice coffee. If he wins, he would sue MacDonald's, Burger King... and be a billionaire. Why did I not think of this? The lady won for the spilling of hot coffee. The jury did not know that eventually we had to pay for all of these and made the lawyers rich. Too many unproductive lawyers makes it tough to operate a business including small businesses. In many countries besides the U.S., the one who sues and loses has to pay for court expenses.

A screener example

The following is an example. Fine tune the selection criteria according to your personal criteria and risk tolerance.

- Bring up Finviz.com from your browser. Select Screener, the third tab. As of 3/24/2015, we have 7066 stocks.

- For illustration purposes, we would like to find stocks with double bottoms, a positive technical indicator. Select the Technical tab. Select Pattern and then Double Bottom. Now we have 257 stocks.

- Select the Fundamental tab that is next to the Technical tab. Select Forward P/E and then select "under 20". Now, we have 86 stocks.

- Select Debt/Equity less than .5. Now, we have 45 stocks. Some industries such as utilities are traditionally high in debt, so you can use 'less than 1'.

- Select EPS growth Q-to-Q over 10%. Now, we have 19 stocks.

- Select the Description tab. Select Country to USA. Now, we have 17 stocks.

- Select Price > 1. Select Avg. Volume "Over 100K". Select Float Short "Under 10%. Select Analyst Recs. "Buy or better". Now we have 9 stocks.

    Now we can evaluate them one by one using Fundamental Analysis, Intangible Analysis, Qualitative Analysis and Technical Analysis. The purpose of screening is to filter the 7000 stocks to a small number (9 stocks in this case).

Skip the stocks that have the Earnings Date within 2 weeks. If you already have too many stocks in the same industry, skip that stock. You can save the screen when you have registered with Finviz.com. It is free. Check the performance of your selections after 3 months or so.

Other sources

Paper trade and check the actual performance before investing your money. Many popular screens provided by many sites worked before but may not work now. It could be too many folks using the same strategy.

Hence it is important to check the current performances of the screen you are using. For yardstick, use SPY or similar ETF that simulates the market. Here are some sources beside Finviz.com.

Your broker

Most broker sites have screen functions. Some have screens to simulate what a specific guru such as what Warren Buffett would buy.

IBD (a subscription service)

From my check on the IBD 50, they're good in the last 10 years, but not that good in the last 5 years – the victim of their own success? They provide stocks from their screens. Most screens are for momentum stocks and large caps. Here are the updated days for specific lists as of this writing.

Stocks Group	Published
Sector Leaders	Daily
Stock spotlight	Daily
Top World	Daily
IBD 50	Mon. and Wed.
Weekly Review	Fri.
Big Cap 20	Tue.

You may want to check out individual stocks with Stock Checkup and then analyze them again. The following are good parameters: Composite Rating, Industry Ranking (finer and better than Sector Ranking) and Relative Price. Understand their parameters and apply accordingly - the same for most other vendors.

IBD prefers large and growing companies with institutional ownership. Some of their parameters may not make sense for small, value and/or turn around companies.

Filler: Irresponsible is my best defense

I told my date that I would not be responsible after the second drink due to the lack of an enzyme.

Common parameters

Different styles of investing use different parameters for screening stocks. Here is my suggested parameters in using Finviz.com. Vary them to your risk tolerance and market conditions. Finviz.com is not complete in all functions, but it could the best free screener that incorporates both the fundamental and the technical criteria. The first table is for Value and the next one for Growth. The last one is for finding stocks that the institutional investors are trading.

Screening value stocks

Value Screens	Common	Penny	Micro Cap	Dividend
General				
Market Cap (M)	>500 M	<50 M	50 -200 M	+Mid(>2B)
Price	>5	< 5	1-15	>5
In all 3 Exchanges	In	Not In	Most are In	In
Avg. Volume	>100K	>5K	>10K	>100K
Country	USA	USA	USA	USA
Dividend%				>3%
Float Short	<10%	<10%	<10%	<10%
Analyst Rec	Buy or +	Buy or + if avail.	Buy or +	Buy or +
Fundamental				
Forward P/E	<20	<20	<20	<25
ROE	>10	>10	>5	>15
QQ earning	>0			>0
QQ sales	>0			>0
PEG	<1	<1	<1	<1.2
Payout%				20-50%
P/S	<10	<10	<10	<10
Technical				
Price above 200 SMA	Yes	Yes	Yes	Yes
RSI(14)	< 70	< 70	< 70	< 70

There may be no analysts or very few following penny stocks and micro-cap stocks. QQ is quarter to quarter.

Screening Growth Stocks

Growth Screen	Common	Technical	Momentum
General			
Market Cap (M)	>50	> 1,000	>500
Price	>1	>10	>5
Exchanges (Major 3)	In	In	In
Avg. Volume	>50K	>200K	>100K
Fundamental			
Forward P/E	<30	<30	<30
Return of Equity	>5	>0	>0
QQ earning	>10%	>15%	>20%
QQ sales	>5%	> 5%	>10%
PEG	<1	<1	<1
Analyst recs.	Buy or +		
Technical			
Price above 200 SMA	Yes	Yes	
50 SMA	Yes	Yes	Yes
RSI	< 75	< 75	

Short-term trends are important for momentum stocks.

Explanation

The above are suggestions only. Adjust them to your personal preferences and risk tolerance.

- Finviz screener lacks ranges, such as market cap and multiple of exchanges. Most Finviz's parameters do not have a range option such as Exchanges, so you need to run the screen three times, one for each of the three major exchanges.

- Average Volume. When the price of the stock is less than $3, double the average volume requirement. In most cases, 10K is quite acceptable to me. When the volume is small, you may have to pay more (a.k.a. spread) to trade.

- There are many fundamental metrics such as Debt/Equity and Price/Free Cash Flow that are not included here, but they should be included in your further evaluation. Each industry sector has different thresholds. For example, the P/S is very different for a supermarket rather than a high-tech company. Compare the company to the average value of the companies in the same sector. Many sites including GuruFocus.com and Fidelity.com have the average values displayed.

- For momentum stock, you can ignore most of the fundamentals and concentrate on the price trend such as SMA-20% (Simple Moving Average for the last 20 trade sessions) and SMA-50%. The higher the percent, the higher it is away from its own average. You do not want to hold momentum stocks too long (max. 3 months unless the momentum is still uptrend); personally my max. is 1 month.

- For growth stocks, ensure the PEG (P/E growth), quarter-to-quarter earnings and quarter-to-quarter sales are above the averages in its own sector and/or the market.

- Technical analysis favors large cap stocks with large volumes. I prefer stocks with positive earnings and they are fundamentally sound.

- When the SMA-20%, SMA-50% and SMA-200% are all positive, they should be in an uptrend.

- RSI(14) indicates whether the stock is oversold (>65) or under bought (<30). The range is my suggestion only.

- You may want to check out your strategies using a virtual account from your broker.

A general guideline for Institutional investors

Criteria	Value
Description	
Relative Volume	Over 2 M
Country	USA usually
Institution Ownership	Over 50%
Technical	
SMA-200	>10%
Volatility	Week – Over 3%
RSI(14)	>40%
Fundamental	
Market Cap	>1B
ROE	>10%

- Again, these are my suggested metrics. I prefer USA companies and many are global companies. If you use foreign countries, ensure they are larger companies and/or in countries that have regulations similar to our SEC's.
- For value investors, select Forward P/E less than 20 (25 for high-tech companies) and their Earnings are positive.
- Check out how many analysts are following the stocks that you are interested in.

To illustrate, I find 12 stocks. I narrow them down to 3. First, I skip all stocks that already have had more than 10% rise recently. They may have risen too high already.

Select profitable stocks with forward P/E less than 25. "Debt/Equity" is less than .5 (50%). Then, ROI is higher than 25%. Stop when you have reached the optimal number of stocks (3 for me in this example).

If you find too many stocks, tighten the criteria and vice versa. Save the criteria and the selected stocks in a portfolio for paper trading.

Links: Basic Finviz https://www.youtube.com/watch?v=cHNUMPgEYGY

Filler: Chicken feet, lobsters and trade war

Lobsters are literally flown to China for the rich. The trade war changes all these. Chicken feet, a delicacy for Chinese, will be thrown to the ocean. I can finally enjoy a $12 plate of lobster in Boston.

Many farmers have gone bankrupted as the banks do not loan them money to buy seeds for the next year. Our storage is over-flowed. Soybeans and pork are rotting. Trump's subsidies will not help a lot for farms who have small farms and he is going to lose all the votes from these farm states.

3   Sectors to be cautious with

There are many reasons to be very cautious when investing in the following sectors. However, Technical Analysis (a.k.a. charting) would give you more hints than the fundamentals for stocks for these sectors. If the big guys are dumping, most likely Technical Analysis (or the simplest SMA-20) would tell you that.

Loan companies/banks

The financial statements do not show the quality of their loan portfolios. Following this advice, you may be able to skip the banks that melted down in 2007. The peak of Citigroup is $550 and several banks went bankrupt.

Many metrics are not relevant for banks such as Debt/Equity and EBIT. The rising interest rate would be good for banks' profits.

Drug (generic is ok)

Understanding the complexities of the drug pipelines, its potential profits for new drugs and the expiration of the current drugs may not worth the effort for most retail investors. In addition, a serious lawsuit and / or a serious problem with a drug could wipe out a good percentage of the stock price. When a drug shows unpromising sign(s) in any trial phase, the stock could plunge and vice versa.

Miners

It is extremely difficult to estimate how much ore (sometimes a miner owns several different types of ores and/or of different grades in the same or different mines) that a company has. It is further complicated by the complexities to extract and transport them. When the total of these costs is greater than its production price, the company will not be profitable. Understanding the market for ore futures is another discipline.

Many mining companies are in foreign countries such as Canada, Australia and countries in South America. Their financial statements of Canada and Australia are more trustworthy than most other emerging countries.

One potential problem of mining companies from many emerging countries is nationalization.

Mining rare earth ore is extremely risky when the profit depends on how China, a major producer of these ores, will price these ores. After China announced the export restrictions on rare earth elements, several non-Chinese companies announced to reopen their mines for rare earths, but few have made any profits as of 2013. Developed countries have stricter environmental regulations.

Coal and eventually oil suffer from the rising use of cleaner energy such as solar and wind.

Insurance companies

Insurance companies profit by:

1. The difference between the total premiums received and the total claims minus expenses in running the company.

2. How well they invest the premiums; you pay your premiums earlier than you may collect from any claims.

They can protect the profits in #1 by restricting claims by natural disasters such as earthquakes and by re-insuring. However, a bad disaster could wipe out a lot of their profits.

Even if the insurance company shows you its investment portfolio, most of us, the retail investors, do not have the time and expertise to analyze it.

Emerging countries (not a sector)

Their financial statements especially from small companies cannot be trusted, and many countries use different accounting standards. Emerging countries are where the economic growth is. I trade FXI, an ETF, rather than individual Chinese companies. I have lost a lot in small Chinese companies due to frauds and politics. To check out whether the stock is an ADR, try ADR.COM (https://www.adr.com/).

Stocks with low volumes (not a sector)

Most likely you pay a high spread to trade these stocks. They can be manipulated easier. I had a hard time trying to sell a stock owned by a few owners.

For simplicity, I trade stocks with the average daily trade volume over 6,000 shares (double it if the price is $2 or less). A better way could be by calculating the percent of your trade quantity / average daily trade volume; it would reduce the effect of penny stocks that have larger volumes due to the low prices.

Good business and bad business
Banking is a good business in a growing economy. My deposit in them makes virtually zero interest, and they loan the same money making 3%. If they are more cautious in loaning, they should make good profits.

Restaurant is an easy business to run, but it is very hard to make good money. With the rising of minimal wages, it will get even tougher. That could be the reason for so many coupons today. The high-end restaurants are doing better due to the rising stock market. The pandemic of 2020 would wipe out a lot of small restaurants.

Retailing is a tough business. Look at the top 10 retailers 15 years ago, I can only find two including Macy's that are still surviving. Most are either went bankrupt or being acquired. Even Macy's was not in good financial shape. Amazon is the killer.

Airlines are a tough business. You can tell by the average increase in fares in the last 10 years. It cannot even beat inflation. They have to charge you for everything. The next frontier charge is the rest room (especially for long-distance flights). Now I understand why they call themselves "Frontier Air". As of 2014, it is quite profitable due to mergers and lower fuel cost. The pandemic of 2020 may be the toughest time for airlines. As of 5/2020, Boeing has many serious troubles and they can only survive with a bailout from the government.

There are several software companies that produce software such as the virus detecting programs and tax preparation software. The customers faithfully buy new versions every year. That's great business.

Afterthoughts
As of 8/2013, is the emerging market oversold?
http://seekingalpha.com/article/1658252-have-emerging-markets-gotten-oversold

When an index of an emerging market is up by 10% and the currency exchange rate to USD is down by 20%, then it is not profitable for us.

4 Fidelity

Fidelity offers a strong screen function. The most unique feature is incorporating its Equity Summary Score (used to be Analyst's Opinion) and some outside researches such as Zacks and Ford.

From the main menu, select "News and Research", "Screen and Filter" and then "Start a screen".

The following example selects stocks with the following criteria: Security Price (2 to 250), Market Cap. (300 and above), Equity Summary Score (8 and above), Zacks (Strongest) and Ford (Strongest).

It displays the 10 stocks. Research each stock. Read the News about each stock. You may want to use Finviz.com, Yahoo!Finance and other sources to double check.

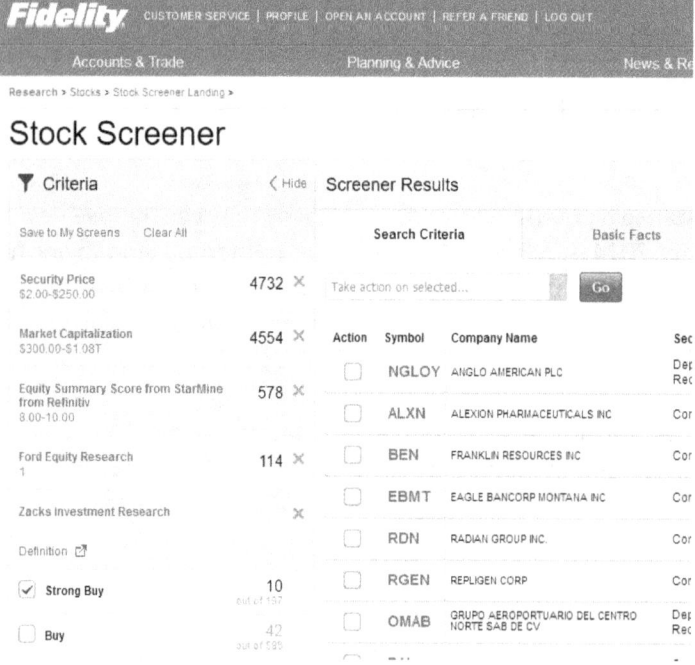

The following describes some of the features.

- Equity Summary Score. It is one of the major metrics I use in my proprietary scoring systems. They are not available to many small stocks. From my limited database in 7/2015 and for short durations, the results are:

Short Term: (7% return for the average)

Metric	Parm. 1	No. of Stocks	%	Parm. 2	No.	%	Predictability
Equity Summary Score	Buy	150	10%	Sell	279	3%	Good

Long Term: (8% return for the average)

Metric	Parm. 1	No. of Stocks	%	Parm. 2	No.	%	Predictability
Equity Summary Score	Buy	90	17%	Sell	208	4%	Good

It has its own limits, but they are very minor to me.

First, it does not have a historical database for verifying the screen performance such as the return after a year. However, I do not know any site that provides this function free. To work around this, I save the results in a spread sheet and update the performance.

Secondly, it does not provide many other filter criteria that can be found in other systems such as technical indicators or insider transactions found in Finviz.com. I use other sites for further evaluation.

Most investors should find that this screening is a very good tool and very easy to use.

5   Performance of my screens

I monitor the performance of my top screens every 6 months or so. Here is my September, 2013 summary. The purpose is identifying the screens that have performed well recently. It is for illustration purpose only. All returns are annualized. They are sorted by Grand Avg. in descending order.

Screen	Last Monitor 2/13	Current Test Avg.	Long-term Avg.	Short-term Avg.	Grand Avg.	Avail.
EP	39%	66%			59%	75%
BB3	35%	70%			53%	25%
LPSER	-21%	72%			49%	75%
MN	19%	53%			45%	75%
CW	64%	49%	39%	20%	38%	100%
LR	30%	37%			35%	100%
TT	30%	26%	71%	8%	35%	100%
TV2	50%	76%	14%	19%	35%	100%
BFSCB	5%	38%			31%	100%
DO	29%	24%	30%		28%	100%
AR	56%	53%	23%	6%	28%	100%
BE	81%	44%	10%	13%	25%	100%
FA	16%	27%			25%	100%
BS5BV	21%	25%			24%	100%
SE		53%	20%	-3%	23%	100%
CAO	-3%	17%	37%	12%	21%	100%
...	...	...	---	...	...	
Avg.	34%	19%	23%	5%	19%	

Screen.
They are the abbreviations. To illustrate, CAO is the screen looking for candidates for acquisition with low market caps. I have about 25 production screens. They have been selected among over 100 screens.

Last Monitor 2/2013.
Copied from the "Current Test Avg." from my last monitor in 2/2013.

Current Test Avg.

It is the average of the four tests on recent months. The four test dates are: 03/11/13 to 7/9/13, 4/9/13 to 8/7/13, 5/9/13 to 8/17/13 and 6/8/13 to 9/6/13. They are about 4 months apart. It is the most important average to reflect what worked recently.

Long-term Avg.
It is the long-term performance (about 12 months) of the actual, screened stocks. These are stocks that have been actually screened and some may have been purchased.

Short-term Avg.
It is the short-term performance (about 6 months) of the actual, screened stocks.

Grand Avg.
It is a weighted average of the above 4 return categories (Last Monitor, Current Test Avg., Long-Term Avg. and Short-Term Avg.) and they're sorted in descending order.

Run the top screens first as they have given me better returns in the past. It does not guarantee that they will perform as well as before, but they have a better chance to perform well than the screens scored below the average.

Availability.
To illustrate, if the screen found stocks in 1 out of the 4 tests, it is 25% available. These screens may not have enough data for prediction on the future results and there is a higher chance that I will not find any stocks using these screens.

Observations
The following are the personal findings on my own screens. You can do something similar to separate your top screens from the rest of your screens. Test and monitor the performances of your own screens.

- Usually the top half of the screens from the last monitor show up in this monitor though their ranks may vary.

- CAO in the last monitor should be better than it indicates. At least two companies had been acquired and they had very good returns. These two companies did not show up in the test as they're taken out from the historical database; it is termed as survivorship bias.

- CW is quite consistent to the last monitor.

- EP and BB3 have not found any stocks in actual usage. MN proves to be a good screen in these two performance monitors. I missed the opportunities to make good money from this screen – my mistake.

- LPSER is a risky screen demonstrated here and from the previous monitors. I prefer not to take unnecessary risk. Include a column of maximum drawdown as it is a good indicator to avoid risky screens.

- LR was below the average and that's why it had not been used. It is above the average in this monitor, so it will be used to some small extent.

- TT is above the average in these two monitors. The returns of screened stocks during this monitor are better in both long term and short term and hence it will be used.

- The original table (not shown here) has comparisons to SPY (an ETF simulating the market). Beating the market is my yardstick. If most of your screens beat the market, most likely they will beat the market again. However, there are exceptions such as when the market is plunging. In this case, value stocks are better than growth stocks, and cash is the king.

  The market during my last monitor is better than this period. If the return of SPY is negative in the last three months, there is a good chance that the market is trending down.

- There are some screens that just do not perform for a long while. They will not even be monitored next time. However, when the phase of the market cycle changes, the performance of these screens may respond differently.

- The test results are not always consistent. It could be due to my limited data, or the market does not behave normally.

Book 7: Evaluating Stocks

The simple formula to make money is to find value stocks and wait for the market to realize their values; it could be a year away. Momentum investors buy stocks that are treading up, and evaluate the purchased stocks again within 3 months. Personally I sell within a month as usually there are better momentum stocks to buy. Only buy when the market is not risky. Aggressive investors find the worst stocks to short. Most successful investors are doing this.

The book value of a stock is simply the net worth of a company (= Assets – Liabilities). When the stock price is higher than the book value per share (i.e. 'Stock Price / Book Price' > 1), it is over-valued. When this ratio is more than 2 or less than 0.5, conservative investors have to be cautious. When it is way underpriced, there may be a critical reason.

Intrinsic Value includes the intangibles such as patents. However, both the Book Value and Intrinsic Value have not been convincing predictors from my tests. I briefly describe some basic but important metrics here.

- Expected (same as Forward) Earnings Yield (E/P). The future appreciation depends on future earnings and the current price of the stock (you do not want to overpay). I prefer a range from 5% to 30%.
- Growth of Earnings and growth of sales. Compare them to their numbers in the same quarter of last year. I prefer 10% or higher.
- How good is the management? It is measured by ROE. I prefer 10% or higher.
- How safe is the company? 'Debt/Equity' is one important metric and Cash Flow is another. The warning sign is that the company does not have enough cash to pay back the debt obligations. I prefer it is less than .5 (same as 50%). However, some industries are debt-intensive.

Most ratios are readily available from many sites including Finviz.com. In most cases there is no need to dig into the complicated financial statements initially. If you do, ensure they are up-to-date. For example, when a stock has a one-to-two split, the price is updated but may not be the Earnings per share, Book per share, etc.

The predictability of most metrics changes according to the current market conditions. Monitor their performance and act accordingly.

How to start

First we filter stocks from about 7,000 selected stocks available from Finviz.com for example; the number is variable from different web sites and/or services. To start with, skip stocks that are not in the three major exchanges, market caps less than 50 M, or daily average volumes less than 10,000 shares.

Check out the "Simplest Way to Evaluate Stocks" in the Common Tools section to evaluate stocks for beginners and couch potatoes. Furthermore, refer to Scoring Stocks to evaluate stocks via a scoring system.

1   Amazing returns

Amazing Returns

To achieve a consistent 10% return above S&P 500 over many years is every fund manager's dream. To double one's investment above the S&P500 return is amazing while tripling it is unheard of. I beat the S&P500 by 700% and I can detail the history of my transactions.

Many analysts show their average yearly returns and/or their returns of their top 10 stocks this time of year. The market has closed early today on Christmas Eve, so I have the time to check my recent performance. As a trader with many trades, it would be far too complicated for me to do the same for the entire year. I selected all the stocks I purchased in the last 90 days. Most of them are deeply-valued stocks. Let's check how I performed so far on these stocks.

Whenever you have achieved a high return such as this one, take the profit as it may have reached its peaks. To me, most profits are made in swing trades with an average holding period of just 90 days.

Stocks bought and their returns as of 12/25/12

Stocks	Date Bought	Return	SPY Return
BANR	12/07/12	3%	-.13%
KTCC	12/06/12	0%	.7%
QCOR	12/07/12	15%	-.1%
KTCC	12/06/12	-1%	.7%
ACTV	12/05/12	-5%	.7%
IAG	12/05/12	-1%	.7%

ADES	12/04/12	6%	.6%
NC	12/03/12	15%	-.3%
VELT	12/03/12	64%	-.3%
ANR	11/28/12	33%	4.8%
AAPL	11/16/12	1%	4.8%
C	11/14/12	13%	3.0%
DECK	11/13/12	16%	2.7%
MSFT	11/13/12	0%	2.7%
ALU	11/13/12	38%	2.7%
DLTR	11/09/12	7%	3.4%
CAT	11/08/12	4%	1.9%
MSFT	11/07/12	-8%	.5%
BSX	10/24/12	14%	.3%
BSX	10/19/12	7%	.3%
20			
AVG:		11%	1.35%

Beat SPY (in %) = (11%-1.35%)/1.35% = 716% or 7 times

Average Return = averaging each return of 20 stocks = 11%
Average Annualized Return = 148% or 122% (= 11% *365 / avg. holding period)
Average Return = Profit / Capitalization = 10%[1]

How the returns are calculated
Using BANR to illustrate how the return and the SPY return are calculated.

BANR	12/07/12	3%	-.13%

BANR was bought on 12/07/12 (17 days from 12/24/12) at 27.93 and it was at 30.43 on 12/24/12.
Rate of Return = (30.43 – 27.93) / 27.93 = 3%

SPY was at 142.53 on 12/07/12 and at 142.35 on 12/24/12.
 Rate of Return = (142.35-142.53) / 142.53 = -.13%

Commissions and dividends are not included for simplicity. Commissions are negligible and dividends could add about another 2% for the annual returns.

Interpreting the performance results
The quantity of each stock bought is not important as I am comparing the return of the stock. However, a few stocks have been listed twice as I

bought two times usually on separate dates. If I chose them as one purchase instead of two, my return would appear even better. The purchases are real, so the amount of each stock is not identical to each other.

I'm not too excited yet. This phenomenal return could be just this one time only. 90 days is a short period. Consistency could be achieved with an improved stock picking technique, plain luck or a combination. By any measure, it is an extremely decent return. However, I do not expect beating S&P 500 by 7 times again.

My best return is from 2009 in my largest taxable account. It was over 80% beating the SPY by about 3 times. 2003 is another good year for profit. These two years are defined by me as the Early Recovery stage in a market cycle and the market provides the best profit opportunity.

The four losers are MSFT (-8%), ACTV (-5%), KTCC (-1%) and IAG (-1%). The best winners are: VELT (64%), ALU (38%), ANR (33%) and QCOR (19%). The following are in a 14% to 16% range: DECK, NC and BSX (2 purchases). Click here for the entire list.

Cheating the results

I could 'cheat' for better results by doing the following, but I did not:

1. Exclude stocks only purchased in the last 20 days (instead of 15).

2. If my purchases of CSCO were included, the result would be even better. CSCO has been bought three times on 7/24/12 and it has gained 31% as of 12/25/12. I still have CSCO, but it is not included as it just hit the 90-days requirement.

3. I could include those buy orders that had not been executed due to their fast appreciation.

Hence, there are many ways to cheat, so you should read others' results carefully.

What stocks were included

There were 20 purchases. I bought some stocks twice and that counted as two purchases. None of the stocks have been sold as of 12/25/12. I have excluded the stocks that I am testing a strategy by trading them every month and most are in a separate account.

How the stocks were picked

The majority of the stocks were screened by my selected screens that had been proven profitable in the last 3 to 6 months, or are historically profitable at this stage of the market cycle. I also analyzed most of the screened stocks and assigned a score (15 and higher is a buy) based on the metrics that had a reliable predication recently. I do not stick with the scoring system 100% of the time, but most of them stocks that I purchased twice have high scores.

The poor performers were scored as: MSFT with a score of 13, ACTV 16, KTCC 27 and IAG 23. The scoring system is OK. MSFT should not be bought judging from its low score. However, I believe MSFT has a long-term appreciation potential. The other three are the latest purchases in this portfolio and they may perform better in a longer period of time.

The winners were scored as: VELT 34, ALU was not scored, ANR was not scored and QCOR 30. The scoring system is great for this group. ALU and ANR were selected from two Seeking Alpha articles and their selections were not based on these scores. I read several Wall Street Journal articles on ALU and CSCO to convince myself to buy both of them.

The average winners were scored as follows: DECK 9, NC 26 and BSX was not scored. DECK was selected based on an article from Seeking Alpha and it seemed DECK was experiencing the same short squeeze as CROX once did. BSX was selected from a Sunday paper article.

Observations

1. I notice that most big winners (ALU is $1) have a stock price less than $10. The myth of holding quality stocks with prices higher than $15 is not true here as most of my big winners were below $10 including ALU.

2. I did not double my normal purchases on VELT and ALU, which both turned out to be my best performers. VELT scored high in my analysis. ALU was very convincing but it seemed to be risky. 'Nothing risk and nothing gained' applies here. I did triple my purchase on CSCO, which is a large company with good fundamentals that were not yet 'discovered' by the market.

Both AAPL and DECK gained more than 25% and then lost most of their gains during my short holding period. I should have sold AAPL as many of my fellow investors sold the winners expecting higher capital gains taxes next year. The myth of 'buy and hold' does not work here.

3. During this period, I had several buy orders that were not executed due to their rising stock prices. Market orders could be the solution. It is another example of pennies smart and a pound foolish.

4. It will be interesting to check the results again in 6 and 12 months. Except ALU, all are in my taxable accounts and I usually keep them for a year to qualify for the lower tax rates due to capital gains.

5. I have not described any specific method, but these concepts help you to build better strategies to customize to your individual situations and/or market conditions. Invest the money you can afford to lose. Past performance does not guarantee future results.

6. Reading articles such as Seeking Alpha can be beneficial providing they are not 'bump-and-switch' scheme. However, you should do your own analysis. It is your money after all.

7. The market has been up by .8% in the last 90 days and this portfolio increased by 11%. If my portfolio amplifies the market, I wonder whether it will be down by the same rate in a down market.

8. This portfolio is quite diversified even that I have not planned that way except weighing more with high tech companies. There are no big winners and no big losers that could change the average returns.

9. I tried not to include emerging countries such as China as I do not trust their balance sheets.

10. I have never achieved such an amazing return. I'm emotionally detached to big wins and big losses. It could be plain luck. Even the best strategy will have its "black swan" moment eventually.

11. To achieve over 100% annualized return is not sustainable by checking the top performers of the S&P 500 index and their returns. However, it is possible but not likely if you churn your portfolio more than once and you time the market correctly.

12. Time to take profits as most stocks here have achieved my objectives. Use the cash to buy stocks with a similar appreciation potential. You will never go broke taking profits.

Conclusion

My three steps of making a stock purchase are: 1. Market timing, 2. Screening stocks, 3. Stock Analysis and 4. When and what to sell. They have all been discussed throughout the book. Market timing and strategy (#2 and #3) does not always work, but it will go better with using them.

I am the living proof *against* the Efficiency Theory and the claims that stock picking does not work. It may not work from time to time, but in the long run it works.

Footnote

[1] Profit / Capitalization should be a little less than 20%. The original 10% is correct when you invest all the 20 stocks at the start of the beginning of the investment period. I bought these stocks on different dates. If I assume the average time of all the stock purchases is at a mid-point, then my average capitalization is only half and hence giving a 20% return.

It is slightly less than 20% as I did not include the stocks that I bought in the last 15 days. Use the number for a comparison and that's why we have to be concerned with the performance from most investment subscriptions.

2   A scoring system

This scoring system helps you to select whether you should buy a stock or not. In this system, when a stock scores higher than 2, it is a buy. As a group, the highly-scored stocks usually perform better than the lowly-scored stocks in a year. The basic concepts are described here.

An Example

For illustration purposes, we use two metrics: Forward P/E and ROI.

First we convert Forward P/E into Forward E/P by flipping the two values. Assuming Forward E/P should have a higher weight than ROI, multiply E/P by 5. The average ROI is 10% (simplified for illustration), so minus it by .1.

   Score = Forward E/P * 5 + (ROI -.1)

For example, a stock has a P/E of 10 (E/P = 1/10= .1) and ROI is expressed as 25%.

   Score = .1 * 5 + (.25 - .1) = .5 + .15= .65

Some parameters by some sites are expressed in grade such as A, B, C and D. For simplicity, if it is A, then the value is 2 otherwise it is zero.

   Score = if (Grade = "A", 2, 0) + ...

Test your system on paper with at least 3 months of data. Check whether your scoring system works. It works when the higher the score corresponds to the better the return. Adjust the weight on each metric and see whether your scoring system improves its predictability.

Again, it is simplified for educational and illustration purpose. Try even more different metrics and check whether the metrics still work in the current market. The next metrics to include could be Equity Summary Score from Fidelity, Debt/Equity and Quarter-to-Quarter Earnings / Sales.

Monitor your scoring system

I am sure that many have tried to use most of the metrics and they still cannot find the Holy Grail. I believe the predictability power of each metric is influenced by the current market conditions. For example, the fundamental metrics such as P/E predict better than the growth metrics such as PEG during the market bottom. You should test the performance of each metric every 6 months or so.

You may have two scores: one for short term and one for long term. The stocks you want to keep in the short term may not be the same kind of stocks you want to keep in the longer term. Short term is 3 months (one month for me) and long term is 12 months for me. My definitions could be different than yours. Value metrics are more important for the long term while growth metrics are more important for the short term.

However, 12 months is too long a period of time and during this period the market may change, so it is better to change it from 12 to 6. To illustrate, energy stocks were great in 2007, but they plunged in 2008. If your scoring system for long-term holding was constructed based on 12 months' data in 2007, the system would have been misleading in 2008 for energy stocks in this example.

I find the short-term scores have a better prediction power than the long-term scores. However, I keep profitable stocks more than 12 months to qualify for the better tax treatments in taxable accounts, and sell the losers less than 12 months. Evaluate the purchased stocks every 6 months to decide whether you want to keep them for another 6 months. Use stops and trialing stops (for winners) to protect your portfolio.

Besides monitoring the metrics in your scoring system, monitor the scores.

The market is not always rational

Sometimes the scoring system fails: When the poorly-scored stocks perform better than the highly-scored stocks. The market is not always rational. Most scoring systems depend on fundamental metrics. When the market switches its favor from value to growth, adjust the score system accordingly. I have found that more than one time that the stocks scored in the top 5% did not perform, so be careful or skip the top 5% (sometimes 10%). The events such as a pending lawsuit or an expiring drug do not show up in metrics, and that is why we need to do other analysis such as Intangible Analysis.

Some metrics almost always work such as the positive predictions of excessive insider's purchases. The insiders know the company typically better than others. When they buy their own company's stock at market prices, they must know it has good appreciation potential. They have many reasons to sell their company's stocks. However, when they sell a large percent of their holdings, be cautious.

When the stock loses more than 30% in a month and you cannot find valid reasons, it may be a good indicator for potential appreciation ahead. Some suggestions are:

- Do not modify your scoring system during market plunges.
- The best strategy is to use the screens (same as searches) that have worked well for the last 90 days.
- Find out why your fundamental metrics that used to work do not work now. You may want to add more weight on growth metrics, and vice versa on value metrics.

An example of monitoring the metrics

This is what I found in monitoring the performances of the metrics as of 3/2013. It is based on a limited database of about 300 stocks with holding periods varying from 1 to 15 months. It has an average of 8% (16% for shorter term). The following is for educational purpose only.

1. The foreign stocks are not doing well: South America (average return is -21% for 7 stocks), Israel (-18% for 2), China (-10% for 7). Europe (0% for 17) and Canada (5% for 16, and most are in natural resources). If I ignore the foreign companies, the return of the portfolio would be increased substantially.

2. The following metrics work fine for the long term only: Forward (same as Expected) Earnings Yield (E/P) and Fidelity's Equity Summary Score.

3. P/B. The stocks with P/B less than 1 perform better than the stocks with P/B greater than 2 (10% vs. 4%).

4. There are no definitive conclusions on Cash / Market Cap, PEG and Return of Equity (a surprise to me) in this monitor.

5. The stocks that were cheaper by 50% to their average 5-year P/E (available from Fidelity) have performed better than those stocks that were cheaper by less than 2%.

6. The ratio of Short / Market Cap between 25% and 30% has better performance than other percentages. It is a contradictory ratio and it

could be a short squeeze (a condition that the stock is running out of shares to sell short).

7. There are many composite scores from different vendors that I subscribe to and they are not disclosed here.

8. Based on the above, I will modify my scoring system. I will still have two scores, one for short term and one for longer term.

Short-term scoring system

The scoring system should work better in the shorter term. For testing this system, I used the above data base, but deleted stocks that have been over 8 months old. It is still a small data base of about 190 stocks.

The result is different from the above as the time frame has been reduced. Here is the summary.

1. The predictability of screens (same as searches) performs about the same as the last monitor. A few screens are better than others. I will not use the under-performing screens with real money.

2. The stock grades from several vendors are not a good indicator this time.

3. Expected (same as Forward) Earnings Yield (E/P) has been a good indicator.

4. Cash Flow is a good indicator (different from the last monitor).

5. Fidelity's Equity Summary Score is a good indicator. Finviz has a similar score, but I prefer to use Fidelity's. Fidelity places higher weight on opinions from analysts that have a better prediction on this stock than others. It eliminates some of the conflict of interest between the analysts and the investing banks s/he works for.

6. The Short Percentage between 25 and 30 is a good contrary indicator (could be a good chance for a short squeeze).

   Its value of less than 10 % is a good indicator. The rest of the range is not conclusive.

7. Cash / Market Cap, Insider Purchase, P/B, ROE and Dividend stocks (>3%) are not conclusive in this monitor.

8. P/S with values less than 0.8 are a good indicator.

9. For some reason I do not know why and how to explain: the top 10% of the top-scored stocks did not perform better than the other stocks that pass.

    It happens in both my two scoring systems. Be suspicious of them and it has happened for more than once. However, the stocks that scored in the bottom 10% are consistently poor performers and that's a good indicator.

There are many other parameters that may be of interest to you. Include them in the performance monitor.

3   Simplest way to evaluate stocks

Beginners should trade ETFs only. This chapter is for the readers who are ready or getting ready to trade stocks. In general, ETFs are diversified, less volatile than trading stocks. However, stocks offer higher profit but higher risk.

Many stock researches have already been done recently and some are available free of charge. I have no affiliation with Fidelity except I retired from it. You can open an account with them with no balance. Their Equity Summary Score is one of the best indicators; I check out **value** stocks with score higher than 8. Concentrate on fundamental metrics such as P/E for long-term holds, and momentum metrics for short-term holds. Add criteria to limit the number of screened stocks. Finviz.com is a free screener.

Several sources

The popular ones are Morningstar, Value Line, The Street and Zacks (currently free for rankings of individual stocks). If they are not free, check out whether they are available from your local library. I have 3 simple ways to evaluate stocks starting with the simplest. In addition, read the articles on the selected stocks from Fidelity, Finviz, Seeking Alpha and many other sources for further evaluation.

Fidelity

Select only stocks that have Fidelity's Equity Summary Score 8 or higher. There are tons of information about a stock. Once a while I did not agree with the score such as SHOP and ZM that scored high in August, 2020. Include the following for your analysis.

A modified stock selection based on a magazine article

Most metrics are available from Finviz except EV/EBITDA.

1. Forward P/E (expected earnings and not based on the last twelve months). It should range from 5 to 15 (10 to 25 for high tech stocks). EV/EBITDA (from Yahoo!Finance) is a better choice as it includes the debts and cash than P/E; it would be more effective if it uses forward earnings. If you do not use EV/EBITDA, ensure Debt/Equity is less than 0.5 except for the debt-intensive industries.

2. ROE (Return of Equity) measures how well the company uses the capital. I prefer stocks with ROE greater than 5%.

3. Volatility. Conservative investors should select stocks with a beta of less than one (i.e. less volatile).

4. Insider Transactions for sales (i.e. negative) from should be less than 5%. If it is -5%, most likely the insiders are dumping it.

5. Compare the metrics such as P/E and Debt/Equity to its five-year average and its competitors (available in Fidelity).

6. Momentum. Check out the SMA-50 (actually SMA-50%) and SMA-200. Ideally they should be positive. SMA-50% is especially important for stocks you do not want to keep for a long time.

7. Check out articles on the stock as some recent events (for example a new lawsuit) have not been included in the metrics.

8. Compare the trend of the sector this stock is in. Under Finviz, enter the related sector ETF.

Summary

The sources are Fidelity (Equity Summary Score and various comparisons), Finviz and Yahoo!Finance (for EV/EBITDA). Value stocks should be held longer.

Category	Score / Metric	Value /Momentum
Score	Fidelity's Equity Summary Score	Both
Value	EV/EBITDA	Value
	P/E cheaper compared to 5-year avg.	Value
	P/E cheaper compared to its sector.	Value
	Insider Purchases	Both
Safety	Debt/Equity	Value
	Compare it to its sector.	Value
Momentum	50-SMA%	Momentum
	200-SMA% (for long term holds).	Value

Articles	Check out latest events	Both
Market	No purchase if market is risky.	Momentum

A simple scoring system using Finviz

Bring up Finviz.com and then enter the stock symbol.

No.	Metric	Good	Bad	Score
1	Forward P/E[1]	Between 2.5 and 12.5, Score = 2	> 50 or < 0, Score = -1	
2	P/ FCF[1]	< 12, Score = 1	>30 or < 0, Score = -1	
3	P/S[1]	< 0.8, Score = 1	< 0, Score = -1	
4	P/ B[1]	< 1, Score = 1	< 0, Score = -1	
5	Compare quarter to quarter of last year Sales Q/Q	> 15%, Score = 1	< 0, Score = -1	
6	EPS Q/Q	> 20%, Score = 1	< 0, Score = -1	
			Grand Score	
	Stock Symbol Date[2]	Current Price	SPY	

Footnote

[1] Negative values for Sales (due to accounting adjustments), Equity and Book are possible but not likely.

[2] The last row is for your information only. SPY is used to measure whether it will beat the market by comparing the return of this stock to the return of SPY.

The Score

Score each metric and sum up all the scores giving the Grand Score. If the Grand Score is 3, the stock passes this scoring system. Even if it is a 2, it still deserves further analysis if you have time. You may want to add scores from other vendors. To illustrate on using Fidelity, add 1 to the score if Fidelity's Equity Summary score is 8 or higher. Monitor the performance after every 6 months or so to see whether this scoring system beats the market.

Very basic advice for beginners

Beginners should stick with U.S. stocks with Market Cap greater than 800 M (million), Debt/Equity less than .25 (25%) except for debt-intensive industries such as utilities and airlines and Forward P/E between 5 to 20 (25 for high-tech companies). These metrics are all available from Finviz.com, which is free.

Do not have more than 20% of your portfolio in one stock (unless it is an ETF or mutual fund) and do not have more than 30% of your portfolio in one sector.

For more conservative investors, buy non-volatile stocks whose beta (available from Yahoo!Finance) is less than 1. Beta of 1 represents the market (the S&P 500 index). For example, a stock with beta 1.5 statistically fluctuates more than 50% of the market and hence it is very volatile.

Try paper trading to check out your strategy and your skill in trading stocks. If your broker does not provide one, use a spreadsheet to record your trades or check the availability of simulator.investopedia.com.

#Filler: Silence is golden

I am glad I did not give advice to a friend who had to decide whether to take a lump sum payment or an annuity. The correction in March, 2020 would wipe out a lot of his portfolio if he took the lump sum payment. No one would share his profits when the predictions are correct, but the blame if it does not materialize.

It is same in investing that nothing is certain. With educated guesses, we should have more rights than wrongs especially in the long run.

Section I: Fundamental metrics

4 Mysteries of P/E

If you believe you can make good money by selecting stocks with low P/Es solely, dream on. If it were that easy, there would be no poor folks. However, buying fundamentally sound companies would reduce the risk and improve the chance of its appreciation.

P/E is the most misunderstood indicator. To me, it is the most useful one among all metrics if it is properly used. Earnings are the key to stock appreciation and P/E measures its value. To illustrate on P/E, you pay a million for a hot-dog cart in NYC. Even if its earnings increase year after year, you will never recoup your investment as you have paid too much even for a good business.

"Buy stocks with P/E below 15 and earnings positive" is not true in many cases. P/E growth (PEG) should be considered at least as a prospect of the company. Many retailers were destroyed by Amazon and many newspapers were destroyed by Facebook and Google. Which sector do you want to buy: the sector in up trending or the dying sector even with a better P/E?

Most old books on value are based on old industries that are no longer applicable in today's market. Read these books but ask the above question.

Better definition
P/E should be inverted as E/P, which is termed as Earnings Yield. Earnings Yield is easy to be compared and understood. It takes care of negative earnings for screening stocks and ranking (comparing stocks with the better P/E first). If you sort P/E in ascending order, your order will be wrong with the negative earnings but right with E/P.

It is usually compared to a 10-year Treasury bill yield (or 30 years) or a CD rate. If the stock has 5% earnings yield and your one-year CD is 1%, then it beats the CD by 4% in absolute numbers and four times better. However, the CD is virtually risk free (with deposit amount limits in most banks). Earning yield is an estimated guess and it may not materialize.

Many ways to predict E/P
- Based on the last 12 months. Project it to the Forward E/P. It is also called the last twelve month E/P.

- Based on analysts' educated guesses. Guesses may not materialize. Based on my experience, the expected usually predicts better than the one based on the last 12 months. This is the one I use most and many investing subscriptions provide this Forward P/E (same as the Expected P/E) or expected E/P.

Usually I do not trust the analyst's opinions due to their conflict of interest. However, the earnings estimate is my exception.

- Based on the last month or the last quarter. Latest information could be better for predictions. However, they are not good for seasonal businesses such as the retail where most sales are done during the Christmas season.
- Besides the Pow PE described later, I take the average of the earnings yield EY as:

The Avg. EY = (EY from the last twelve month + Expected EY + EY from the current month of prior year) / 3

It averages out using figures from the past, the present and the future. If no one has used it, I claim shamelessly it is my original idea.

Best E/P could not be the best

Very high E/P could be signs of troubles ahead such as a lawsuit pending, fraud, etc. If you find companies E/P over 50%, it means two years' profits could be equal to the entire cost of the company! I can tell you right away that they probably smell fishy unless you believe that there is a free lunch in life.

However, from time to time, some bargains do exist due to certain conditions, or the Wall Street is just wrong about the company. I found one in my year-end screen and that gave me huge return. You need to find out whether they are bargains or traps. When the E/P is low (sometimes even negative) but is improving fast, it could mean big profits for you. Fundamentalists may miss this opportunity in the early stages due to the unfavorable E/P, but it could be the most profitable time to buy. Sometimes, it could be a turnaround.

During a recession, most good companies have a hard time in promoting new products as the consumers are thrifty. At the same time, it usually is the best time to develop products if they have enough cash to finance them. In this case, there will be no alarm even with negative earnings. The only alarm is when a company cannot meet the debt obligations.

Some companies can manipulate earnings via dirty tricks in accounting. It could make this year look really good, but it is harder or even impossible to continue the same trick for many years. Check out the footnotes in the financial statement.

E/P and PEG

For value investing, E/P is usually used and the higher the better. Watch out when it is extraordinarily high.

PEG (P/E growth) measures the rate of improving P/E. '1' is supposed to be neutral to most investors. When it is below 1, it is undervalued, and vice versa.

PEG = (P/E) / Earnings Growth Rate

They have a similar problem with P/E with negative earnings.

Which of the following two stocks do you want to buy based on their historical earning yields and earnings growth?

1. A stock that has a 10% earnings yield with no earnings growth.
2. A stock that has an 8% earnings yield with 50% earnings growth.

If the earnings growth continues, in next year the second stock should pay 12%, substantially better than the first stock. This is another reason we should use forward earnings rather than historical earnings.

PEG may give a low value for companies that pay high dividends. To correct it,

PEG = (P/E)/ (Earning Growth Rate + Dividend Yield)

When the general market favors growth stocks, weigh more on growth metrics including PEG. I claim no credit on the adjusted PEG.

Fundamental metrics

E/P is one of the metrics you should use but not exclusively. If the earning yield is high but the % of debt is high too, then a good bargain may not be as good as it appears to be.

Some other metrics may not be easily found in the financial statements such as the intangibles, insider buying, pension obligations, trade secrets, losing market share, brand name, customers' loyalty, etc. It is interesting that most metrics change its ability to predict from time to time.

P/E variations

There are other P/E variations like Shiller P/E (same as CAPE and PE10). Shiller P/E can also be used to track the current market valuation. It is controversial and its value is easily misinterpreted. Hence, use it as a reference only unless you understand all its issues. I prefer to use two year average of the P/E instead of 10 as I believe the market changes too much over a ten year span. Currently Shill P/E does not work that well as before. It is due to the excessive printing of money.

Compare a company's current P/E to its average P/E in the last 5 years. Also compare it to the average value of the companies in the same industry. The average P/E for high-tech companies is different from supermarkets for example. They are available from Fidelity.

P/E is more reliable for a group of stocks (SPY for example) instead of individual stocks which have too many other metrics and intangibles to deal with. When you compare the total return of an ETF to a corresponding index, you need to add the respective dividends to the index to ensure a fair comparison of total returns. As of this writing, the S&P 500 is paying about a 2% dividend.

EV/EBITDA is another way to measure the value of a company. This metric has its advantages and disadvantages over P/E. It includes other important data such as cash and debt. EBITDA/EV is equivalent to E/P including other mentioned metrics. I prefer to use it over E/P. Some sites do not provide it if the earnings is negative. The disadvantage to me is it does not use expected earnings. This ratio can be found under Yahoo!Finance.

Garbage in, garbage out
I do not trust most financial statements from emerging countries, especially the smaller companies. Watch out for fraudulent data. Most metrics can be manipulated. Recently I have a US stock that lost 18% in one day due to the SEC's investigation of its financial data.

The announced earnings may not be reflected in the financial statements that you use from the web. Ensure your data is up-to-date by checking the date of the financial statements. Seeking Alpha has transcripts for the earnings announcements that would save you a trip to attend the companies' quarterly meetings.

Sector and entire market
You can find the value of a sector using the P/E of an ETF for that sector. It is similar for the market. For example, use SPY (an ETF simulating the S&P 500 index). If it is lower than the average (15 to me), then most likely the market is good value and a buy signal. It is one of the many hints for market timing.

Where to use P/E
Each highlight of the following corresponds to one of my books. Click it for the description of the strategy.

My book on top-down approach starts with a safe market, then sector analysis, fundamental analysis, intangible analysis and optionally technical analysis. P/E is one of the many metrics in fundamental analysis.

There are many styles of investing. In general, fundamental analysis is important when you hold the stock longer.

- P/E is important in Long-Term Swing, Dividend Investing, Retirees and Conservative Strategies.
- My max value is 20 and 25 for tech companies. I ignore it if they have high potential for appreciation that could be indicated by insider purchases. However, many unknown companies then had a P/E over 50. Tesla had a P/E over 1,000 at one time.
- P/E is moderately important in Short-Term Swing and Sector Rotation.
- P/E is the least important in Momentum Strategy and Day Trading.

Summary
Again, one metric should not dictate the reason to trade a stock. Compare the company P/E to its industry average and its own five-year average. In addition, many industries have cycles. If you buy it at the peak of the industry, the P/E may mislead you. Besides fundamental analysis, you need to consider intangible analysis and time the entry / exit point by using technical analysis. Intangible analysis evaluates information that cannot be summarized into numeric metrics such as a lawsuit pending.

True P/E
"EV/EBITDA" is available from Yahoo!Finance and other sources. The true EY is "1/Ture PE". I call it "True" for the lack of a better term as it represents

the financial situation of the company better. This could be the most important metric for many.

Earnings can be manipulated. For example, the company management can lower the P/E ratio by buying back its stocks. In this case the earnings per share is boosted but in reality there is no change in the company's financial fundamentals. The true P/E takes into consideration the reduced cash. EBITBA stands for "Earnings Before Interest, Taxes, Depreciation, and Amortization".

Be careful when EV or "EBITDA" is negative. Most likely you should avoid the stocks with a negative EV.

Yahoo!Finance usually leaves EV/EVITDA blank for financial institutions such banks, loan companies and REITS. In this case, use forward earnings yield (= 1 / Forward P/E or Pow Earnings Yield described next.

Pow P/E

You should use the described "EV/EBITDA" and hence "Pow P/E" can be ignored. There are some cases that Pow P/E is better: 1. "EV/EBITDA" may not be available for reasons such as negative asset and 2. Use of Forward Earnings instead of Earnings based on the last twelve months. The following is an exercise on how I simulate it from Finviz.com with metrics that are readily available.

I modified P/E to take care of cash and debts. I use my last name due to being easier to distinguish from P/E and it has nothing to do with my ego.

Pow P/E = (P - Cash per Share + Debt per Share) / (Earning - Interest gained per share - Interest paid per share)

Pow Earnings Yield = 1 / Pow P/E

Here is a comparison of E/P (Earnings Yield), Expected Earnings Yield (Forward E /P), True Yield (EBITD/EV) and Pow Earning Yields, which is based one Forward (Expected) Earnings as of 10/14/2021.

	CARS	MPAA
Earnings Yield	1%	7%
Expected Earnings Yield	12%	12%
True Yield	13%	11%
Pow Earnings Yield	5%	9%

P/E is not always important

The following is my test from 1/2/2020 to 10/14/2020. RSP is similar to SPY except that the stocks in the S&P 500 index are equally weighed. EY (= E/P) is Expected Earnings Yield and there is no stocks with EY less than 0. DY is Dividend Yield. GPE is the growth of P/E. As in my book, I use annualized returns and dividends are not included. This test does not mean a lot, but it tells us what these metrics behave during this period, or it indicates **Value is not a good metric in this period**, and it may indicate momentum Is better in this period. Most big winners start as small companies with **high P/E** (from 30 to 100). Many of them have important technologies or special systems that would change the world such as Microsoft, Facebook, Amazon and Walmart to name a few. Their sales have increased substantially year after year.

Examples of not depending on low P/Es. Before the financial crisis in 2008, P/Es of most bank stocks had 10-year low. After they announced the earnings, P/Es of many of them surged to over 100 and the stock prices suffered losses of more than 80% within 12 months. The stock price of Bethlehem Steel with P/E of 2 at one time went to zero. Need to find out why the stock is so cheap via intangible analysis and qualitative analysis.

The following is very rough testing and there are many limitations in the database. However, the conclusion is quite convincing to me and some are opposite to the contrary beliefs. For example, I expected the higher EY the better, but not in this test.

	Ann. Return	Indicator	Comment
RSP 500 All	-2%		
EY (top 10)	-54%	Bad	Contrary
GPE (top 10)	-20%	Bad	Contrary
Select All or top 100.			
DY = 0	16%	Good	
DY (top 100)	-19%	Bad	
DY / 1 and 2	2%		
EY 3 to 4	15%	Good	Second best
EY 2 to 3	6%	Good	Third best
EY 1 to 2	31%	Good	Best
EY 0 to 1	-39%	Bad`	

I use some metrics from a service I subscribe to that are not included here. Two major metrics of this subscription have a return of around 20%. Most subscriptions including the free Fidelity (to some extent) give you three composite scores: Total, Fundamental and Timing. I wish to check out the recent predictability of Fidelity's Equity Summary Score if they have a historical database. Most of them take out the delisted and /or bankrupt companies in their databases.

Link: P/E: https://www.youtube.com/watch?v=4KkTGx2bK_4

5 Fundamental metrics

ROE

Return of equity (ROE = Net Income / Equity) could be the most important financial indicator to determine how well the management is doing their job. However, in recent years, this metric has been overused and loses its prediction reliability.

The company's return on equity for at least the last five years would indicate how the stock price endures major financial downturns as well as upturns.

Comparing the ROE to the average ROE for the sector is a good indicator on how well the company is managed compared to its peers. Some sectors including utilities have low average ROEs.

Market Cap (Capitalization)

Market Cap = Total no. of outstanding shares * share price

I recommend the beginners buy U.S. stocks with a market cap greater than 800 M (million). Here are the current conventions (everyone's convention is different) and they should be adjusted to inflation.

Class	Market Cap (million)
Nano Cap	< $50M
Micro Cap	$50M to $250M
Small Cap	$250M to $1B (billion)
Mid Cap	$1B to $10B
Large Cap (Blue Chip)	$10B to $50B

| Mega Cap | >50B |

The higher the cap is, usually the less risky the stock would be. Nano Cap and Micro Cap are reserved for speculators or owners of the companies. Small Cap and Mid Cap are for knowledgeable investors as most institutional investors would skip these stocks in these caps especially Small Cap. Large Cap, Mega Cap and some Mid Cap are the stocks traded by institutional investors. They are thoroughly researched continuously.

My metrics

My current favorites are Forward P/E, PEG, Fidelity's Equity Summary Score, Short % of outstanding shares, Free Cash Flow, ROE and Debt Load / Equity.

In addition, I use many summarized metrics from different sources. For example, one of my subscription services gives me a composite rank for fundamentals and another one for momentum. To illustrate, click here for Blue Chip Growth which is no longer free for stock analysis. Enter IBM as the stock symbol. As of 2/2013, it gives C for a Total Grade, D for Quantity Grade and B for Fundamental Grade. The Total Grade is usually a composite grade of other grades.

Use the metrics to screen through the stocks to reduce the number of stocks for further consideration.

Mid, high and low values of common metrics

Metric	Mid Range	Low Range	High Range
P/E (last 12 months)	< 10	>40	< 4
Price / Cash Flow	< 12	>30	< 4
Price / Sales	< 2.5	>3	< .2
Price / Book	< 2.0	>4	< .2
PEG	< 1.5	>2	< .2

High Range means good values (although in this table it means low numbers), but sometimes it is too good to be true. Low Range means bad values. To illustrate, many internet stocks in 2000 had P/E over 40 (bad) while a neglected bargain stock has a P/E of 3 (supposed to be good). A bargain could also mean they could have some hidden problems. In reality, I prefer the Mid Range. Using P/E to illustrate, it should be between 4 and

10. Adjust the range according to your personal tolerance and the current market conditions. If the market trend is up, you may want to relax the range to 5 to 12 for example otherwise you cannot find too many stocks for further evaluation.

These values are my selections based on data for about 10 years. They are used for predicting the performance of a stock in a year; review the ranges every 6 months in the current market.

The metrics with the high-range and mid-range values offer better predictions for the stock price appreciation. From the above table, the stocks with the low-range values have a better chance than other stocks to lose money in a year or so. Some favorable numbers could be high values instead of low values such as ROE.

However, the range values could change. When the market favors momentum or you do not keep stocks for less than a month or so, the momentum metrics including PEG and price growth could be better predictors. We need to check to see whether the current market favors which metrics: Value or Growth – some websites and subscription services identify the current favorite. In addition, the performance of each metric should be evaluated every 3 to 6 months. In addition, new range values need to be adjusted with the above table.

Fundamental metrics take a longer time (about 6-12 months vs. 1 month for momentum metrics) for the performance to materialize. The metrics in the above table besides PEG are all fundamental metrics. Except for financial stocks, P/B is always worthless.

Examples of searching with high range values

Stocks with low-range values for most metrics (such as 40 in P/E in the above table) could be risky. Hence, select the stocks with the mid-range value (e.g. 10 for P/E). Avoid the low-range values indicated by the metrics.

Here is one example of selecting stocks with high range values of P/E and P/B. Most likely, you will not find too many stocks with these criteria.

$E > 0$ and
$P/E < 4$ and
$P/B < .2$

E is earning per share and we need the company to be profitable.

High range values could indicate something is wrong with the company, e.g. a lawsuit pending. I would consider a P/E of less than 4 is suspicious. However, very small companies are often neglected by the market, so they could be solid companies. Don't forget to do your due diligence and spend more time in thoroughly evaluating the stock and its industry.

The stocks with the low-range values have a greater chance of losing money in the next year or so. That is proven statistically as a group despite some exceptions. AMZN[2] is not a valued stock by its high P/E or its high P/B. However, if the company is investing for the future by building infrastructure and capturing the market share, you may ignore these unfavorable metrics. Personally I prefer fundamentally sound companies today.

Note. P/B is not a good metric for established companies and / or companies with a lot of research such as IBM. Many metric formulae are outdated due to ignoring intellectual properties, patents and market appeals such as brand names.

Example of a search for mid-range values

E > 0 and
P/E < 10 and
P/E > 4

In this case, you only include companies with positive earnings and P/Es within the range from 4 to 10 exclusively. You should find many companies with the mid-range values of P/Es.

Add other filters such as minimum price, market cap and average volume. If you do not find too many stocks, relax your criteria (start with mid-range values in the table), and vice versa to limit the number of stocks. If you usually find stocks with a screen but not today, it usually means that the market is overvalued and that you cannot find many bargain stocks.

Again, it is the first step to narrow down the number of stocks to be analyzed. Your metrics will not cover stocks with special situations. For example, IBM always has had a high Price/Book value for as long as I can remember and therefore it does not mean it should be excluded.

The searches based on fundamental metrics help us to narrow stocks for further evaluation. Occasionally I abandon the scoring system for some stocks under special conditions.

Compare a company's metrics to its sector's averages
This could be the most powerful comparison: Compare Apples to Apples.

You may want to compare the metrics of a company to the averages of that sector. The average of supermarket's P/S is extremely low and hence it has no meaning to compare a supermarket's P/S to most other sectors. Some sectors like utilities need high debt to run a utility company.

However, when the average P/E or other metric of a sector is suddenly lower than its historical average, it could mean that sector is out-of-favor and/or the sector is having a better value.

This following table compares Apple to its sector and a retail sector on a specific date for illustration. All the metrics will change.

Metric	Apple	Computer	Retail
P/E	11	19	24
(5 year average)	16	17	15
PEG	.6	N/A	1.4
Price /Cash Flow	9.4	8.1	9.2
Price /Book	3.3	3.0	3.6
EPS Growth	-6%	-42%	2.6%
(last 5 years)	62%	45%	11%
Operating Margin	20%	15%	8%
ROE	30%	14%	19%
Debt / Equity	2%	7%	88%
Inventory Turnover	76%	53%	4.55x

From the above table, some metrics only make sense for an industrial sector (Computer for Apple). In this case, you may want to compare AAPL to Computer, and not to Retail.

"Debt / Equity" indicates that the retail sector needs to borrow more than the computer sector for example. Of course retail stores has high Inventory Turnover.

Top down approach

First, compare whether the market is risky. Second, select the best sector; there are many sites including Finviz.com to select the best sector. Then compare the fundamental metrics of the major stocks within that sector.

Some metrics do not apply

Using financial institutions as an example, usually P/B is more useful than P/CF. However, the quality of a loan (not a metric here) is more important than all metrics as we found out in 2007. P/S is more important for retails. However, the expected P/E is most important for most other sectors.

When you believe a sector is the currently best (a criterion available in many screeners), select the best stocks in this sector.

Compare metrics to its five-year average

If the company's five-year average of P/E (available from Fidelity and many other sites) is 20 and today it is 10. It is 100% under-valued by this standard. Also, you may want to try other metrics such as debt/equity and compare it to the five-year average.

Growth Metrics

The growth metrics are growth rates of the stock price, sales, earnings, etc. They are useful for growth investors.

Even for value investors, the earnings growth rate is very important, as most stocks with substantial gains have increased their earnings growth first. If the earnings has grown but the price remains the same (i.e. PEG), then the potential for price appreciation will be higher and most likely it will return to the historical average P/E.

Momentum Metrics

Momentum metrics is part of growth. The rates of increase of the stock price, the volume... are the major metrics. Earnings revision is another one especially in earnings announcement seasons (usually 4 times a year).

Fidelity and many subscription services provide a composite rank with name Timely or similar name. The following could be part of this Timely score: SMA-50, Q-Q sales increase and recent price appreciation. In my momentum portfolio, I use these metrics and ignore all the other metrics as my average holding period is less than 30 days for momentum strategies.

Insiders' buying

Insiders sell their stocks for many reasons. When insiders buy a lot of their companies' stocks at market prices, take notice. Insiders know better than anyone about the health of their companies and their industries.

Select Insiders' purchases from one of the available sites such as Finviz.com. Ignore the option exercises. I prefer the high ratios of Net Total Purchase Value / Market Cap and the purchases by more than one insider. Be careful that the insiders purchase the stocks after selling a similar amount of stock in a brief time span.

OpenInsider is a good site for this info.
InsiderSights is a good one too with more capable tools that would take more time to learn.

Where to get the metrics
You can get this information from the website with no or low cost such as Finviz.com, your broker's site, AAII (very low cost) and Fidelity.

The following subscriptions are at a little higher cost but they are still less than $1,000 per year: Value Line, IBD, Zacks, VectorVest and Stock Screen 123. Many data from different vendors are duplicated such as P/E. You will save time by concentrating on one or two sources.

Many vendors provide a composite metric such as a value metric to cover P/E, debt... and a timing metric to cover Technical Analysis indicators, PEG, price appreciation rate...

Short % is a useful metric available in Finviz.com. For Fidelity customers, you can click on Research and then Stock. Enter the stock name, and then click on Detailed. I find Fidelity's Analysts' Opinions quite useful.

Finviz.com provides a lot of useful information free of charge. It also provides a screen function. The 'Help' button describes Finviz's functions and all the metrics monitored.

Other sources are: Insider Cow, NASDAQ Guru Analysis ...

Monitor the recent performance of the metrics
The predictability of most metrics has proven not to perform consistently as many investors and fund managers found out. My theory is that the

specific metric works better in some market conditions than others. To test which ones work better currently, check their performance in the last three months and use those that perform well. This is what my scoring system in the book Scoring Stocks is based on.

Why some metrics fail sometimes
Most investors are using metrics to screen stocks, but few are successful consistently. Some investment companies have top analysts dedicated to projects looking for the right strategy. My guesses why they fail are:

1. Metrics need to be monitored to see its effectiveness on current market conditions.

2. Besides fundamental metrics, there are many intangibles.

3. When they have too many followers on the same metrics, they will not work such as ROE in the last several years.

4. Fundamentals need time (at least 6 months) to reflect the value of the stock. You're swimming against the tide as a fundamentalist. Trading momentum stocks using basic fundamentals will not work.

5. Watch out 'Garbage in and garbage out'. Some emerging countries do not have an organization similar to SEC to ensure the integrity of the financial statements of a company and some audit firms are being paid to cover their eyes. Even though there are frauds in some U.S. companies and with their auditors.

6. The metrics may be derived from obsolete financial statements. Check out the date. The most updated one could be available from the company's website.

7. Some companies borrow a lot of money to dress up the metrics such as P/E and ROE. They will look good short-term but not long-term. Ensure the debt/equity has not been increased recently for this purpose. I recall one utility spin-off had incredible fundamentals except the debt load. It is so high that all these fundamentals will deteriorate in the future due to servicing its high debts.

Footnote

[1] The stocks are classified into sector and then sectors are divided into industries (same as sub sectors). For example, oil is a sector and oil

exploration and oil services are industries under the oil sector. For simplicity, I intermix the terms here as many sectors do not need further sub classifications for this discussion.

[2] AMZN is not a value stock by any standard. As of 1/1/2013, its P/E (from last 12 months) is 157 and P/B is 15. Both fall far into my low-range values. Its price rises from 256 from 1/1/13 to 270 today (1/22/13). Today its P/E is ridiculously over 3,000. The investors are betting AMZN's internet sales will take over the concrete stores and its investors do not care about profit but rather for market share. Does it sound familiar in the internet era? Its price momentum is indicated positively by any chart. It may be a good stock for traders, but it is too risky for a swing trader and a long-term investor like me (yes, I wear two hats). I do not short stocks in a rising market, but this could be an exception.

Afterthoughts

- The only recommendation from a very popular investment book I read is to select stocks by the return of equity (ROE). I will save you the time and money to read that book. I read the entire book in an hour at Barnes and Noble's and it saved me some money / time, not to mention cutting down trees for that book. Basically it does not work today.

- DAL has an interesting Debt / Equity of over -1000% due to the negative equity. For a comparison, you may want to use Debt / ABS(Equity).

- Once in a while, I found the financial data was not consistent from different sources. Try to check out any discrepancy in the dates of the financial data of your sources. The financial statements from the company websites usually have the most updated data.

- Current Ratio = Current Asset / Current Liability. If it is below 1, then the company is having a tough time in meeting its current cash obligations.

- Dividend Yield is a valid metric for matured companies. I do not use it to evaluate growth companies or companies that need to plow back cash for research and development.

- If you use Finviz.com, you find three margins: profit, gross and operating. I prefer to use profit margin that is more useful for most companies. The other two may be relevant in some sectors.

  http://www.investopedia.com/terms/p/profitmargin.asp
  http://www.investopedia.com/terms/g/grossmargin.asp
  http://www.investopedia.com/terms/o/operatingmargin.asp

  Use Wikipedia for more description.

- Enron had millions in profits but negative cash flows. Earnings can be manipulated but not the cash flows.

  Insiders' selling usually does not cause any alarm unless excessively. Most insiders sell most of the stocks they have before these companies go bankrupt. Just common sense!

- Why fundamentals are important.
  (http://seekingalpha.com/article/1612442-its-shorting-season)

  On the same day when this article was published, RVLT was up 10% due to increasing sales in the earnings conference. However, the company is still not profitable. It shows how tough shorting is even with good arguments. That's why do not expect every purchase is profitable. However, with the educated guesses, you should beat the market in the long run.

- Due to my ignorance, limited time or my short period of holding stocks, I have not used intrinsic value that often.

  Book value is different from intrinsic value. Book value is calculated by summing up the values of all pieces of a company such as a building and all equipment.

  Intrinsic value is the real value of a company. When two companies have the same book value and market cap, the company that generates more profit than the other one usually has a higher intrinsic value. When the intrinsic value is higher than the stock price, it is underpriced in theory.

  The following link provides more info on intrinsic value.
  http://en.wikipedia.org/wiki/Intrinsic_value_%28finance%29

6   Finviz's parameters

Most metrics are described in Finviz (via Help), Investopedia and/or Wikipedia and my chapters on P/E and fundamental metrics if available. We use the metrics for screening stocks and then evaluating the screened stocks.

The following are my personal comments and why I feel some metrics are more important than the others. Personally I divide the metrics into fundamentals and technical, which are more important for long-term investors and short-term investors respectively.

Compare the ratios to the companies in the same sector (industry) and also its averages from the last few years (5 preferable) from many other websites such as Fidelity.

From your browser, enter Finviz.com. Enter a symbol (I used ABEO for discussion). A chart is displayed with the prices and volumes for the last eleven months. SMAs (Single Moving Average) are displayed sometimes with other technical indicators. Intraday, Daily and Weekly options are available for day traders, short-term traders and long-term traders respectively.

Besides the chart and the metrics described next, it describes what the company does, analysts' recommendations (I prefer Fidelity's Equity Summary), insiders' trading and articles that are good for intangible and qualitative analysis. Many free websites such as Yahoo!Finance may provide a list of articles about the company.

"Financial Highlights and Statements" are materials for more in-depth analysis and they were more important decades ago when most financial ratios had not been calculated for you. It is important for investors with good knowledge in financial accounting. The current version also includes basic financial statements and cash flow for the current (TTM) and the last two years.

A section on Insider Trading is also included. Do not be alarmed when insiders dump small quantities of the stocks. Buying large quantities (e.g. insider transaction more than 5%) at prices close to the market price could be favorable news.

The following metrics are roughly based on the flow of Finviz from top to bottom and left to right. I skip those metrics that I believe are not too important. You can also place your cursor on the metric to retrieve the description from Finviz. Some metrics are left blank to indicate they are not applicable (zero, negative or not available). For example, the Debt/Equity of YRCW in 1/2019 is blank (same as null) due to its negative Equity. From Yahoo!Finance at the time of writing, it has a total debt of 888M.

- **Index**. Most of us trade stocks in the three major exchanges in the USA. Stocks listed over-the-counter are too risky for most of us. Skip the stocks in local exchanges and foreign exchanges unless you are an expert on these stocks and/or have insightful (not insider) information. I screen the stocks and then ignore the stocks that are not in the Dow, NASDAQ and Amex. Other screeners may let you select a group of exchanges.

- **Market Cap** (MC). To me, stocks below 50M are risky even though they could be very profitable. Ensure the Avg. Volume is at least 10,000 shares and / or your order is less than 1% of the average volume. Some small stocks are controlled by the owners and have small volumes. In this case you cannot sell your stock easily.

    Float = Outstanding shares – Insider shares.

    Usually Float does not matter as they are typically the same. However, it does for small companies with large insider shares. Most of these owners do not want to sell their family businesses and hence they reduce the chance of being acquired entirely or partially for good prices. In this case, you may have to hold this stock for a long time or you sell it at a very unfavorable price.

- If **Forward P/E** (a.k.a. Expected P/E) is not provided, use the P/E which is based on the trailing last 12 months (TTM). Alternatively, calculate the E by using the E from P/E and multiplying it by its growth rate. It may not be seasonally adjusted. I prefer using Forward P/E as it provides a better predictability power to me.

    Finviz.com leaves the P/E blank (same as null) if the earnings are negative. In this case, I would check out Yahoo!Finance's EV / EBITDA, which also considers taxes, cash and interests. The blank condition is similar to some metrics such as when the asset is negative (they seldom occur).

Earnings Yield is equal to E/P. I call it True Earnings Yield for EBITDA / EV. It is easier to understand. Compare Earnings Yield or True Yield to the annual dividend yield of a 10-year Treasury – with the low interest rate in 2021, skip the comparison.

E/P is easier in screening and sorting the screened stocks. If you use P/E instead of E/P, you need to screen or sort stocks with a clause "P/E > 0".

When the P/E is less than 5, be careful and there may be a reason why it is so low. Many bankrupting companies have low P/Es at one time.

Compare the P/E or Forward P/E with the average P/E for the sector and its average P/E for the last 5 years that are available from Fidelity.com. Some sectors have high P/Es. If the sector is cyclical, the earnings could be affected.

When the prospect of the company is good such as Tesla in 2020, ignore P/E.

- **Cash / share**. It is used to calculate Pow P/E and Pow EY when EV/EBITDA for the stock is not available. To illustrate, if the stock is $10 and it has $10 cash / share without debt (i.e. Debt/Equity = 0), most likely it is underpriced as you can get the whole company for nothing. You should find out why the price is so low. It could be the market ignoring the stock, or there is a serious event happening such as a major lawsuit.

- **Dividend %** is useful for income investors. The payout ratio should not be more than 30% except for matured companies. Most developing companies plough back the profits into research and development, and hence they do not pay dividends.

- **Recs**. Select stocks with 1 or 2. Do not base your stock selection on this recommendation alone. There have been many bad recommendations that could cost you a fortune in losses. Use Fidelity's Equity Summary Score instead.

- **PEG** is a measure of the growth of P/E and hence a growth metric. It is similar to P/E, but it takes the expected earnings growth rate into account. The lower value is better as long as earnings are positive. If earnings are negative, then the reverse is true. It is a defect in using P/E and PEG and that's why I recommend EY (Earnings Yield) and EYG, earnings yield growth.

If there are two companies with the same P/E, the one with a better PEG ratio is better. If two companies have the same E/P, the company with higher Earnings Growth (EPS Q/Q) would be better for similar logic.

- **P/B**. Book value (= Total Assets − Total Liabilities) may not include intangible assets such as patents. Do not trust it 100%, so is ROE which is based on the book value. Negative equity is possible when Total Liabilities is more than Total Assets. This popular metric is outdated for most matured companies as it is now made up of more intangible assets including patents, management, the quality of their employees, brand names, market share, partners, free cash flow and customer base.

- **P/S**. If two companies are unprofitable, this ratio can be used. A retail company such as Walmart is very different from a research company. This metric is only meaningful for stocks within the same sector or specific sectors.

- **P/FCF**. I prefer it to be greater than 0 and less than 50 for value investors. Most metrics can be manipulated easily, but not this one.

- **Sales Q/Q** reduces the seasonal deviation. To illustrate, retail sales for the Christmas season should be compared to the same season in the prior year.

- **EPS Q/Q**. Same as above. I prefer the growth of EPS over Sales. Both of these Q/Q ratios are growth metrics. When a company terminates its unprofitable product(s), its Sales Q/Q could be down but its EPS Q/Q could be up. In 2000, many internet companies had great Sales Q/Qs but negative EPS Q/Qs.

Q/Q comparison (quarter to quarter) takes out the seasonal variations as Sales Q/Q. I prefer both Sales Q/Q and EPS Q/Q increase. When EPS Q/Q increases far higher than Sales Q/Q, it could mean the EPS Q/Q could be temporary such as the oil company when the oil price rockets.

When the company buys its own shares, EPS could be misleading as E is fixed and the number of shares is reduced. In most cases, the fundamentals of the company have not changed.

- Positive **Insider** Transactions are favorable. Sometimes, they are misleading. Need to scroll to the end of the screen and check out more info there. If the transactions are outdated such as 3 months or so ago, and or they are purchases in a similar amount than the sales a while ago, they are not important. Insiders know the company better than us. So is Institutional Transactions as institutional investors move the market.

- Insider Own, Shares Outstanding and Shares **Float** determine the number of shares that are available for trading. A small Float with a high Insider Own limits trading and the stock should be avoided in most cases. Compare your trade position for the stock to the Avg. Volume.

- **Profit Margin**. I prefer it over Gross Margin and Oper. Margin which does not include interest expenses and taxes. When you sell software, the Gross Margin is high as it does not include development, support and marketing, etc. A retail store has low Gross Margin. It all depends on the industry, and hence it is better to compare companies in the same industry.

- **Short Float**. I prefer it to be less than 10%. If it is greater than 10%, the shorters could find something wrong with the company. If it is over 25% (indicating a possible short squeeze), I would check the fundamentals. If they are good, I would buy expecting a short squeeze potential. It is risky but it has been proven to be profitable for me.

- Technical metrics: SMA-20, SMA-50 and SMA-200. Finviz expresses them in convenient percentages. If they are all positive, it means the trend is up. SMA-20 and SMA-50 are a short-term trend and SMA-200 is a long-term trend. If you are a short-term swing investor, stick with the short-term trend and vice versa. The first two are also used as momentum grades. Many long-term investors do not buy stocks when the SMA-200% is negative.

- **RSI(14)**. If it is greater than 65%, it is overbought. If it is under 30%, it is under-bought for me. Some use 5% up or down than mine. Use it as a reference. Most stocks making new heights are always overbought, and many of these stocks keep on rising. I recommend using trailing stops to protect your profit.

- **Beta.** A volatile stock fluctuates a lot. It is good for short-term traders. A beta of 1 means the stock would fluctuate with the market, and be volatile if it is higher than 1. For volatile stocks (higher than 1), the stops should be higher. For example, if your stops are normally 15%, you may want to use 20% or even higher.

- Management performance is measured by <u>ROE</u>. It is also judged by **Analysts' Rec.** and Institutional Ownership (except for small companies). The confidence of their own ability, the company and its sector is measured by Insider Ownership and Insider Purchases.

    ROE = Net Income / Average Shareholder's Equity
    According to Investopedia, a normal ROE for utilities should be 10% while high tech companies should be 15%. Compare this ratio and many other ratios with its peers that are available from Fidelity.

- Avoid all companies that are going to bankrupt at all costs. Debt/Equity, P/FCF, Cash/Sh., P/B, Profit Margin, Forward P/E, Short Float, RSI(14), SMA20% and SMA50 would give us hints. Need to summarize all the info and study many other factors such as obsoleting products (including drugs).

- Unless you have concrete information, do not buy stocks a week or so before the Earnings Date. It is seldom to make great profits when the announcement is better than the expected.

More useful information:

- The price chart. It has a lot of features such as the resistance line. Some charts include technical indicators such as double top (a bearish warning) and double bottom (a bullish sign).
- Description under the symbol. It briefly describes what the company (sector and industry) does and its country of registration. You want to buy a stock within a sector that is trending up. For example, according to Finviz Apple is in the Consumer Goods sector and the Electronic Equipment industry.

    If you do not want to buy foreign stocks, skip it if it is not listed in the US exchange.

- Articles on the company for qualitative analysis.
- Insider trading. Pay more attention to the insider purchases at market prices. Use common sense.
- The last line lets you open Yahoo!Finance and other sites.

Other important sites

Yahoo!Finance.

From Statistics, you can find Enterprise Value / EBITDA. I call it True Yield when I flip them to EBITDA / Enterprise Value.

In case it is not available, I use Earnings Yield. In my spreadsheet without considering the cell designations,

=IF (Earnings Yield = "", True Yield, Earnings Yield)

Fidelity

Compare the P/E of the average PE of the last 5 years. In my spreadsheet for demonstration,

Cheaper By Historically =IF(PE="","",(Avg. of 5-year PE -PE)/Avg. of 5-year PE)

Compare the P/E of companies in the same sector. In my spreadsheet for demonstration,

Cheaper By To the peers =IF(PE="","",(Industry PE - PE)/Industry PE)

Your broker's website

Your broker website should have plenty of tools to analyze stocks. As of Dec., 2018, Fidelity lets you use their extensive research free by opening an account with no position restriction. I describe some of their metrics that should be beneficial to your research.

- Equity Summary Score. Potentially good buy when it is 7 (8 for conservative investors) or higher. With some exceptions, you should avoid or short stocks if the score is 3 or below. The stocks ranking from 4 to 6 could be turnaround candidates if they are supported by good Q/Q Earnings and/or good news.

- The 5-year averages are good yardsticks. For example, in Dec., 2018, C's P/E is about 9 and the average is 14. Hence it is a value buy.

Other sources

If you have other sources (most require a subscription or being a customer), skip the stocks that have one of the failing grades. The exceptions are a new positive development and increased insider purchases.

Vendor	Grade	Fail
Fidelity	Equity Summary Score	< 7
IBD	Composite grade	< 50
Value Line	Proj. 3-5 yr. return. Also its composite rating	< 3%
Zacks	Rank	5
VectorVest	VST	< 0.7

You may be able to find Value Line and IBD in your library. Try out the free stock reports from your broker first. Finviz and Seeking Alpha should have articles (now fewer free articles from Seeking Alpha) on stocks and earnings conferences, which could have important information after separating from the "welcome" and garbage talks.

Yahoo!Finance has good info. "EV/EBITDA" is better than "P/E" as it considers debts and cash. Most use Earnings from last 12 months, which has poorer predictability than Forward Earnings to me.

When negative values such as Equity in Finviz.com, we need to adjust many related metrics or do not use them at all.

MarketWatch.com has many articles on the market in general and personal investing.

If the stock is close to the Earnings Date (found in Finviz.com), you should avoid trading the stock; as earnings could have a big swing for the stock price. Consult Zacks' ranking which is currently free for individual stocks.

Gurus

It is nice to know how gurus would rate the interested stocks. GuruFocus is a good source. NASDAQ is a simplified version, but it is currently free. Bring up Nasdaq.com from your browser. Select "Investing" and then "Guru Screeners". On the third selection, enter the stock symbol such as THO. Click "Go". You will find how 10 or so gurus would evaluate this stock in theory. Click "Detailed Analysis" for each guru.

Quick and dirty

Many times we need to evaluate a stock fast such as taking action due to some development. Refer to my other article "Simplest way to evaluate stocks". The following should take a few minutes. Bring up Finviz.com and enter the stock symbol.

Using SWKS on 6/10/16 to illustrate, Forward P/E is about 11 (fine between 3 and 25), Debt/Eq. is 0 (fine less than .5), ROE is 30% (fine greater than 5%) and P/PCF is 31 (fine if not negative).

Also, check out Market Cap, Avg. Volume, Dividend, Short Float (fine between 0% and 10%), Country and Industry. Judging from the above, it is a buy.

If you have more time, check out the following: Recom. (Ok if less than 2.5), P/B (fine between .5 and 4), Sales Q/Q (fine if not negative), EPS Q/Q (fine if not negative), Cash/Sh (compare it to Debt/Sh) and Profit Margin (fine >5%). Check some articles described for this stock.

5-minute stock evaluation

It takes even less time than the above "Quick and Dirty". However, I recommend you should spend more time researching stocks.

- From Finviz.com, enter the stock or ETF symbol. Look at the number of reds in metrics. If there are more than greens, most likely it is not a good stock.

- It should be fine if Fidelity's Equity Summary Score is greater than 8.

If you have more time, I recommend you to check the following:

- Check out Forward P/E (E>0 and P/E < 20), Debut / Equity (< 50%) and P/FCF (not in red color).

    If time is allowed, replace Forward P/E with True P/E (same as "EV/EBITDA"), which is available from Yahoo!Finance and other sources.

- SMA20 (or SMA50 for longer holding period). If SMA20 is > 10%, it is trending up.

- It is fine if the Insider Transaction is positive.

- Be cautious on foreign stocks and low-volume stocks.

- If most of the above are positive, it is likely a buy. As in life, nothing is 100% certain.

Links
PEG: http://en.wikipedia.org/wiki/PEG_ratio
Short %:
http://www.investopedia.com/university/shortselling/shortselling1.asp#axzz2LNDvpemo
Openinsider: http://www.openinsider.com/
Finviz: http://Finviz.com/
terms: http://www.Finviz.com/help/screener.ashx
Insider Cow: http://www.insidercow.com/
Current Ratio: http://en.wikipedia.org/wiki/Current_ratio
How to find quality stocks.
http://seekingalpha.com/article/2381395-how-to-identify-quality-stocks-and-is-there-really-alpha-to-be-had

Section II: Beyond fundamentals

Buy stocks based on appreciation potential, not based on when and what you traded the stock for.

7   Intangibles

I give a score for each stock I evaluate. Occasionally some stocks with poor scores have great returns and vice versa. In general, the scoring system works. It has been proven statistically and repeatedly from my limited data. I stick with high-score stocks with some exceptions.

Once in a while I change my scoring system to adept to the current market conditions. To illustrate, the market bottom phase and early recovery phase of the market cycle favor value more than momentum/growth. Here are some of my recent experiences and strategies:

- I double or even triple my stake on stocks with high scores. In the longer term, they are consistently better winners than the average with some minor exceptions. Besides the score, look at the intangibles described in this article.

- Watch out for the stocks with outrageous metrics such as P/E of 4 or less. It could be a big lawsuit pending, an expiration of some important drugs, etc. Also, be careful with scores in the top 5%. From my statistics they do worse than the average. Their problems may not show up in the current financial statements.

- The technology of a tech company cannot be ignored even though the company's P/E is high, that I set a limit of 25 instead of 20 for other stocks. The value of the company's technology and patents will not be shown in the fundamental metrics except from the insiders' purchases at market prices.

    For example, IDCC rose about 40% in 2 days. There was a rumor that Google was buying the company and/or Apple was bidding on it too for its mobile technology. Charts usually would flag this kind of event. For non-charters, use the SMA-20% from Finviz.com. They could be a little late as the charts depend on rising prices.

- There are more acquisitions during a market bottom (same as early recovery). The companies with good technologies are bargains and the larger companies especially those in the same sector understand their values better than most of us. These potentially profitable companies will not be shown by their scores explicitly. When corporations have a lot of cash or the credit is cheap, they are looking for smaller companies to acquire or invest in. The candidates are usually small, beaten up, low-priced and having valuable intangible assets such as technologies, customer base and/or market share of the industry segment. 2009-2012 was just the perfect environment and the before that was 2003. I had at least one stock in each of these periods and they appreciated a lot.

- The opposite is Netflix, Chipotle in 1/2012 and Amazon in 1/2013. They are over-priced by any measure. However, the mentioned companies are investing in the future. The shorters (not for beginners) are having a tough time in making money on them. When their P/Es are higher than 40, watch out. Some could be OK in the mentioned companies, but usually they are not. Do not follow the herd and your due diligence will verify whether they will still go up.

  Use reward/risk ratio. It is based on experiences. To illustrate, if the company has the equal chance to go up 50% and go down 25%, then it is a buy and the reverse is a sell.

- The retail investor just cannot possibly know about some events until they actually happen. For example, ATSC dropped 15% due to losing its second primary customer. Fundamentals cannot predict this kind of events. Charts can signal this event, but usually they are too late unless you watch the chart all day long.

- After a quick run up, TZOO plunged due to missing some negligible earning expectations. It seems the original climbing prices already had the perfect earnings growth built-in.

  I do not understand why a company loses 10% of its market cap when it missed by 1% of the expected earnings. It could be driven up and down by the institutional investors. Evaluate the stock before you act. Acting opposite to the institutional investors could be very profitable for the right stocks. Avoid trading before the earnings announcement dates (about 4 times a year for most stocks).

- The following are not easily found in financial statements: industry outlook, patents, good will, market share, competition, product margins, management quality, lawsuits pending, potential acquisition, pension obligations, advertising icons, etc. That is why we need to read articles on the stocks in our buy list or our purchased stocks.

- The financial data could be fraudulent or manipulated. I do not trust small companies in emerging markets. I have been burned too many times. Check the company names such as foreign names, ADR and their headquarter addresses (from the company profile in most investing sites).

  Earnings can be manipulated with many accounting tricks. A jump in earnings from last year may not be as rosy as it looks. Check the footnotes in the accounting statements. I usually skip financial statements unless I have big purchases in mind as my time in investing is limited.

- Cash flow cannot be easily manipulated. It is good information whether the company will survive or not, but to me it does not prove to be a consistent predictor in my tests, but an important red flag for companies on their way to bankruptcy. Examples abound.

- Repeated one-time, non-recurring and extraordinary charges are red flags.

- Stay away from the companies where the CEOs are over-compensated. As of 7- 2013, Activision's CEO raised his salary by more than 600%, while the stock lost its value in double digits.

- Value stocks. Need to know why they become value stocks (i.e. fewer investors want to own) even they are financially sound. For example, there are two primary reasons for the downfall of a supplier to Apple: 1. Apple is declining in sales and 2. Apple is switching suppliers to replace their product. Technology companies are continually building better mouse traps. They could turn around in a year or so with better products.

Conclusion

Buying a stock is an educated guess that its stock price will rise. Fundamentals do not always work, but they work most of the time:

1. When we buy a value stock, we're swimming against the tide. Hence, we need to wait longer (usually more than 6 months) for the market to realize its value. The exception is the Early Recovery phase (see the Market Cycle chapter) and it has faster and larger returns than most other stocks from most other stages of the market cycle.

2. Some metrics are misleading. Book value could be misleading for an established company such as IBM. The image of the cowboy in a tobacco company could be a very important asset that is not included in its financial statement.

3. The market is not always rational.

Afterthoughts

- Brand names of big companies are one of the most important intangibles. Here is a strategy to buy big companies in a down market. It has been proven that it works. However, do not just buy these companies without analysis.
  http://seekingalpha.com/article/1324041-buying-brand-names-in-a-bear-market-can-make-you-rich

- The reputation of a company takes a long time to build but a bad incidence to destroy in the case of GM such as the delay in recalling the killer switches.

#Filler: Carrie Fisher, another sad American story

Unless drug addiction is part of the culture now as evidenced from the legalization of certain drugs, we're in a permissive society! Brits pushed opium as a nation when they had nothing better to trade. Opium killed millions of Chinese and bankrupted China. When we do not learn from history, we will repeat history. It is another sad story of fame and money and then losing it all. I bet she would be happier in a normal life instead of being born in a privileged class. Same can be said for many celebrities such as Presley, Houston and her daughter. RIP.

8 Qualitative analysis

This is the last analysis to evaluate a stock fundamentally. Then the next is technical analysis which is used to find an entry point (also the exit point) for the stock. The market is not always rational. It also depends of the available of money such as easy credit to pump up the market.

Where quantitative analysis fails and why

I find that some stocks with high scores fail and some stocks with low scores succeed as indicated by my performance monitor. The scoring system still works statistically for the majority of my stocks.

- Reasons why stocks with low scores perform:

  - Over-sold. The institutional investors (fund managers and pension managers) dump them first, and then followed by the retail investors. These big boys will buy these stocks back when they reach a certain price range. RSI(14), a technical indicator described in the Technical Analysis article and is available from many sites including Finviz, is useful to detect these over-sold stocks. I use 25 or below (some use 30).

  - The falling price (P) improves all fundamental metrics that have the stock price such as P/E and P/Sales. However, the trend of the price is down. Improving Forward P/E is usually a good hint.

  - The company has turned around after fixing its problems and/or the market has changed for the better. A new management team could improve profitability such as recalling Steve Jobs for Apple.

  - The current problems have been resolved but not known to the public that could be evidenced by the increase Insiders' Purchases (from Finviz to start). It includes resolving a lawsuit, a new product, a new drug, or a new big order, etc.

  - Heavy purchases by insiders. The company's outlook is not shown in its financial statements. Sometimes the insiders hide them so they can buy more of their companies' stocks for themselves.

- Reasons why stocks with high scores plunge in addition to the described in the previous discussion:

    - The company's fundamentals and its prices have reached or closed to the maximum heights. They have no way to go but down. It is particularly true when the stock's timing rating is at or close to the highest point. TTWO that I gifted to my grandchildren had been 5-baggers in the last few years before it plunged in 2018.

    - It has reached its potential value (or a target price) and it is time for many investors to take profits.

    - Sector (or finding another stock or sector with better appreciation potential)) rotation, particularly by institutional investors who drive the market.

        - The outlook of the company, its sector and/or the market is deteriorating. Most companies with P/E less than 5 have problems, and you need to find out the reasons why the stocks are so cheap. Via Finviz, check out debt / share (more than 0.5), negative Q-Q Sales, negative Q-Q Profits, and/or outdated products like typewriters.

    - The stock price may be manipulated. There are many reasons to pump and dump the stock. Shorting is not recommended for most investors. However, some experienced shorters make money consistently when they find valid reasons to short stocks.

    - It could be due to a new serious lawsuit, a new competing product or drug, canceling a major order, etc.

    - Downgrade by analysts. They could spot some bad events such as product defects, violations of regulations or accounting errors / frauds. The downgrades are more important than the upgrades that could have conflict of interest.

    - The financial statement had been manipulated. The SEC may ask for an investigation.

    - Does not meet the consensus in earnings announcements, which have been over-acted by many investors.

Qualitative Analysis

We need to do further analysis after the quantitative analysis and the intangible analysis. Check out the company's prospects. Check out the date of the article and any potential hidden agenda items from the author. Older articles may not have much value.

Be careful on 'pump-and-dump' manipulation written by authors with a hidden agenda. It has happened especially on small companies before even SeekingAlpha.com has its share. Here was an article that tells you to sell NHTC. There was another article to tell you to buy ARTX. They fit into this category.

The sources are:

1. Seeking Alpha.
   Type the symbol of the company to read as many articles on the company as you have time for. Today this site and many other similar sites require you to be a paid member. If you cannot find too many good articles, check out the articles from Finviz.com.

   Recently, I read an article on AMD and it said it may have good profits in the next two years with the game consoles. The outlook of a company is not shown by any fundamental metric which are far from favorable.

   Following a well-known writer, I bought IBM without doing my due diligence (my fault). It went down more than 15% quickly. You can learn from my mistakes.
2. Research reports from your broker. If you do not find many, open an account with one that provides such reports. Some subscription services such as Value Line provide such reports.
3. Yahoo!Finance board. Most comments are garbage. However, once in a while you find some great insights. Usually you cannot find any info from other sources on tiny companies.
4. The most recent company's financial statements. They are usually available in the company's web site.
5. 10-Ks from Edgar database (www.sec.gov/edgar). Check out new products and its potential competition, key customers, order backlog, research and development and pending lawsuits.
6. Check out the outlook of the sector the company is in and the company itself.
7. Check out its competitors.

8. Some companies are run by stupid people. I received information via my email saying that my mutual fund account could be treated as an abandoned property. I have been cashing dividend checks every year and why it would be considered as an abandoned property. I called them right away to close my account.

   The tall and handsome guy presented articulately how he would turn around JC Penny on TV. I could tell you right away that all his tricks had been tried by other companies such as Sears, and most did not work. The intelligent investor does not care about how handsome, how articulated, how rich his family is and how many advanced degrees from prestigious colleges he possesses. If he does not make sense, do not buy his preaching and his company's stock. [Update. As of 5/2020, J.C. Penny filed for bankruptcy protection. If you had this stock and my book, you would have saved a lot of money minus $10 for my book!]

9. Check out its business model. Some business models do not make business sense and some do. Here are some samples.
- Giving razors makes sense, as the customers have to buy the blades eventually and keep on buying blades for life.
- Supermarket M lowers prices on common merchandises such as Coke and it works. They make money by providing inferior (but profitable to them) products that you cannot compare prices easily such as meat and seafood.

   Eventually there will be a supermarket in my area to satisfy me both in price and quality or at least make a good tradeoff.
- Last week it had been brutally hot. I went to a Barns & Noble's bookstore to enjoy reading the updated books and enjoyed the air conditioning. When there are more free loaders like me than customers, this business model does not work.
- Market dumping works to capture the market. Microsoft used to do it with their new Office and Mail products that could not compete with the established products at the time. Google is following the same model to dump its equivalent products to compete with Office. Now, Microsoft is taking a dose of the same medicine. As of 2015, Google is not winning.

   Amazon.com gives writers (like myself) great deals if you only sell your digital books via them. This model will work so far, as it has captured the self-publishing market today.

9   Avoid bankrupting companies

Avoid the bankrupting companies at all costs. Here are some hints that a company is going bankrupt:

- I had several companies that had lost most of their stock values. It turns out that most were Chinese companies. I did have some losers from Mexico, Israel and Ireland. I believe most were set up to cheat investors. Most if not all had 'rosy' financial statements. Avoid them, especially small companies in emerging countries.
- Many U.S. companies failed due to fraud, poor management, and/or the management betting wrongly. When the CEO is using the company as his own AMT, or having an extravagant life style, watch out. If they promise you a return doubling the current rate of return of the market, listen to your wise mother: there is no free lunch. Despite so many real examples, still fools are born every day, because greed is a human nature.
- Do not follow the 'commentators' on TV. They have their own hidden agenda which usually is not in your interest.
- Many companies fail due to their lack of ability to pay back their loans. Except for specific industries and situations, avoid companies with high debt (Debt/Equity over 50%). Financial institutions and companies that have high debt in order to finance their products for their customers such as utilities are the exceptions.
- I have a screen named Big Losers beating the market by more than 600% in Early Recovery (a phase defined by me). However, some bankrupted companies are not included in the database which is termed as survivor bias. Hence, the actual result is far worse than the 600%. I still use this screen but skip these companies using the following yardsticks.
    - The companies are usually safe with high Free Cash Flow / Equity and high Expected Profit / Stock Price.
    - The following are red flags: low Free Cash Flow / Equity, high Inventory and high Receivable (esp. relative to its Payable), high P/B (over 30) and high net Debt/Equity (over 1 to 3 depending on the industry).
    - P/PFC should be greater than 0 and less than 50. A healthy cash flow may not be able to service the debt if it is too huge. Hence, compare it to Debt/Equity. Compare the cash flow per year to debt obligations per year.
- New government regulations could bankrupt an industry. What would happen when the U.S. takes out the rebates and subsidies of solar panels? When the U.S. banned solar panels from China, one of my

Chinese stocks went bankrupt. Also government bailed out bankrupting companies such as Chrysler (that I made a good profit) and AIG Fannie Mae in 2008.
- Serious lawsuits- Most U.S. companies are required to file this information in their financial reports.
- Obsolete products. Newspapers, retail and similar products would be replaced by the internet. The opposite is new products such as virtual reality products.
- Many companies run out of money during the development phase of the major products. Many are too optimistic in their business plans.
- If you expect the market will recover in 2 years, ensure the company's cash and net income can support their burn rate for at least two more years.
- Many investing sites (most require subscriptions) have safety scores.
- If the Beneish M-Score is greater than -2.22, the company is likely an accounting manipulator.
- Choose companies with Z-Score higher than 3; it does not applicable to financial companies. Both M-Score and Z-Score are available from GuruFocus, a paid subscription. Z-Score does not work for financial institutions.
- Z-Score metrics are: "Working Capital / Total Assets" (A), "Retained Earnings / Total Assets" (B), "Earnings Before Interest & Taxes / Total Assets" (C), "Market Cap / Total Liabilities" (D) and "Sales / Total Assets" (E).
Z-Score = 1.2 A + 1.4 B + 3.3 C +.6 D + E
- Market timing- It does not always work, but it is far better to follow a proven technique than not. It is far safer to take money out of the market when the market is too risky or is plunging. The big losers are companies that provide non-essential products in a down turn.
- Small companies could be risky but very profitable. Typically they have a low stock price (less than $5), small market cap (less than 50 M), low sales (less than $25 M) and low institutional ownership (less than 5%).
- Avoid companies when their own bond ratings are not equal to AAA or AA (www.moodys.com).
- The fall of a sector such as oil in 2015 could drive the related companies, or even a country to the brink of bankruptcy.

Investing is risky to start with. However, investing especially in stocks has been proven to be the best vehicle to beat inflation.

Book 8: Strategies

A strategy starts with when and what stocks to buy and ends with when and why you wants to sell your stocks. This book outlines some simple strategies.

1 Super long-term investing

I am more a value investor than a growth investor. The difference between the two is keeping the stock longer for value investing (a year to me). A growth investor weighs the momentum metrics (such as SMA) more than fundamentals. A growth investor would rotate stocks and/or sectors more frequently (one to three months to me).

Usually I sell my value stocks after they satisfy my objectives, and the holding period is about a year. I seldom have stocks appreciated more than 100%. Some did more than 100% due to many factors such as not reviewing my portfolio early enough, holding them less than 1 year in my taxable accounts or being merged.

Recently, I discovered my TTWO has appreciated 6 times in last 6 years from May, 2015 representing 100% appreciation per year. It proves 'never sold' is a good strategy too, if there is a good reason. The reason on this stock is gaming would be big for our generation, and it is very hard and expensive for new comers into games.

The fundamentals of TTWO were not fantastic in 2015, and that was the reason I bought it so cheap. Many analysts thought the stock would not perform after its franchise game. If there is a good reason, contrary investing could be profitable.

For some reason not disclosed here, I cannot place a stop order to 'protect' the gain. I am sure it would be stopped out using trailing stops. If I use stops on this stock, I would use 20% on the current price and review the stop periodically (say monthly). There are some companies that will be impacted severely such as the internet, green energy and electric cars.

I should use the same strategy in many of my value stocks, and I hope to report more of them in the future. That is the reason why some investors are very profitable, even their portfolios lose more than 50%. We should let the winners rise and the losers out.

2 How to hedge inflation

Inflation is caused by a lot of cash chasing a limited number of products. Major causes for our inflation:

- Excessive printing of money.
- Tariffs especially on Chinese import products.
- High national debt.
- The pandemic slows down factory output.
- Infrastructure.

To illustrate, Australia raises the price of iron ore that causes China to raise the price of steel. China also cuts down the export of their steel to the U.S., which requires a lot of steel for the infrastructure projects. The best way to raise money to pay for the steel is printing more money. The cycle is repeating itself. I have recommended the following ETFs to hedge inflation in my books.

Commodity	ETF
Gold	GLD
Silver	SLV
Commodity	IYM
OIL	USO

Personally I bought minors ETFs such as RING and COPX, and the mining stocks such as FCX and NEM. ETFs are less risky in general. As of 6/2021, they have been performing well. Hopefully they will offset my losses in contra ETFs; I did not expect our leaders printing money excessively to save the market. It is better to hold stocks of companies such as those producing staple products than the depreciating USD.

The Fed has been reluctant to raise interest rate. It would hurt the housing market and the stocks making big-ticket products such as cars. We have a record-high margin level. When the market has a minor correction, margin calls will happen, and the snowball effect would bring down the market as explained in the following links.
https://www.youtube.com/watch?v=37aP94Kw-y8
https://www.youtube.com/watch?v=NEX_Qt7cJdM

3   Making 20% return year after year

This web article (https://www.youtube.com/watch?v=G9xVNjJBSzg) is interesting. Most ideas have been described in this book. I include their pointers here with my own comments:

1. Invest, not speculate. Treat your stock as a company (Buffett's idea). Buy low and sell high. No need to watch your stock every day. Review it periodically by following articles on the stocks you bought via Finviz.com and many other sources.
2. Avoid fees. Broker commissions are free from many sources such as Fidelity. Do not invest via hedge funds. If you do not have time for research, buy an ETF such as SPY.
3. Value investing. You only sell when it has met your investing objective, and/or the fundamentals of the company have changed for the worse. Use Fidelity's Equity Summary Score. Do not buy stocks with the score less than 7 unless you have good reasons.
4. Buy below intrinsic value. Forward Earnings / Price (> 5%) is a good measure with low Debt / Equity (< .5 with some exceptions for industries that require high debts) and no Insider dumping (> -10%). They are all available from Finviz.com.
5. Be patient. Value stocks need time (a year or more) for Wall Street to recognize their values.
   Accumulate cash when the market is risky and expensive. Practice market timing that would tell you to exit the market when the market is plunging.
6. The market is not efficient, and hence blind investing needs to losses usually. It means the market could be over-priced or underpriced. When the P/E of SPY is over 18 (from ETFdb.com), most likely the market is over-priced.
7. Have plenty of cash or liquidity. Hence you are ready when opportunity comes (similar to Rule #5).
8. Average down only if the fundamental metrics agree. I do not average down with some exceptions such as GameStop. Many stocks go bankrupted, averaging down could amplify your loss.
9. Rebalance your portfolio. Do not have more than 30% of your portfolio in one sector. With the exception of sector ETFs, most ETFs have diversified into many stocks with various sectors. I prefer 10 stocks or 5 for smaller portfolio. Check out the stocks you own periodically (a month or more frequently depending on your time available. Finviz should have many articles on your stocks.
10. Know what you are doing and be consistent. Knowledge is important.
11. I add the following rule: Do not afraid of high flyers or stocks making new highs. Protect your portfolio with stops.

4   Insider Trading

Investopedia defines it as:

"Insider trading can be illegal or legal depending on when the insider makes the trade: it is illegal when the material information is still nonpublic-- trading while having special knowledge is unfair to other investors who don't have access to such knowledge. Illegal insider trading therefore includes tipping others when you have any sort of nonpublic information. Directors are not the only ones who have the potential to be convicted of insider trading. People such as brokers and even family members can be guilty.

Insider trading is legal once the material information has been made public, at which time the insider has no direct advantage over other investors. The SEC, however, still requires all insiders to report all their transactions. So, as insiders have an insight into the workings of their company, it may be wise for an investor to look at these reports to see how insiders are legally trading their stock."

If you need more information, click this link from Wikipedia.
http://en.wikipedia.org/wiki/Insider_trading

My additions to conventional insider trading

Hopefully my additions improve the performance of this strategy that has already been proven to work most of the time.

- I add market timing to Insider Trading. You need to sell most stocks except contra ETFs before or during a market plunge and buy them back as indicated by the chart; I provide a simple marketing technique without charts.

- Diversify your portfolio. Keep 10 stocks for a portfolio less than a million. Ensure that there are not more than 3 stocks in the same sector. Keep 20 stocks for portfolio over a million. Too many stocks would require more of your time that would be better spent in evaluating individual stocks. However, keeping too few of stocks would impact your portfolio when one stock has a big loss.

It is just a recommendation. Vary your holding size and holding period according to your time, your portfolio size and your knowledge in investing.

- Stick with stocks over $2, average daily volume over 12,000 shares (8,000 for stock prices over $20) and market cap over 200 million.

    Most big winners usually are in the price range between the $2 and $15 price and market cap between 200 million to 800 million. They represent the stocks that institutional investors are ignoring due to their restrictions. This is just a general guideline and there are always exceptions. Change them according to your requirements.

    I prefer to skip stocks from most emerging countries, especially the smaller companies, as I do not trust their financial statements.

- Ignore the subscription services or books claiming they are making over 30% consistently. Some even have examples of making 5,000%. Most likely they tell you their winners but not their losers. It is easy to pick up winners that fit their strategies, but they do not tell you the real performance.

    Check whether their portfolio uses cash, as it cannot be manipulated such as using the best prices of the day to trade. I bet that most portfolios consistently making over 30% are not real. Alternatively, they have 10 portfolios, and they only show you the one that makes a good profit.

    When they back test their strategies, they cheat their performances with survivor bias (i.e. those bankrupt stocks are not in the historical database). If their returns are that great, do you think they will share their secrets with you?

5   Dividend Investing

Basic ratios for dividend stocks

- **Ex-dividend date**

You will be eligible for dividends if you have your stock on the record. You want to buy the stock earlier, or on ex-dividend date in order to receive the dividend.

- Payout Ratio

It is the dividend / profit. Too high a ratio may not be good as the company does not plow back the profit into research / development. Most mature companies have higher payout ratios as they do not need to plow back into research / development compared to high-tech companies.

The other option of using the company's cash is in a stock buyback that would increase the stock values in theory.

Earnings per share = Earnings / Outstanding Shares.

When 'Earnings' is fixed but Outstanding Shares are reduced, the ratio looks good deceptively. The management do this often as it would boost the values of their options.

- Dividend Yield.

It is dividend / price.

Why companies pay dividends

Companies can use the profit by plowing back cash into research / development, buying back its stocks, acquiring companies and/or giving dividends to the stock holders. In theory, the company should consider the option most beneficial to the average stock holder. In practice, the management tries to benefit themselves by choosing the option best to appreciate their stocks and hence the stock options they own.

My additions to conventional dividend investing

Hopefully my additions would improve the performance of this strategy.

- I add market timing to dividend investing. You need to sell most stocks before a market plunge and buy them back as indicated by market timing indicator.

- Diversify your portfolio. Keep 10 stocks for a portfolio of less than a million dollars. Ensure no more than 3 stocks are in the same sector. Keep 20 stocks for portfolio over a million dollars. Holding too many stocks would require more of your time that would be better spent in evaluating individual stocks. Holding too few stocks would impact your portfolio when one stock has a big loss.

  It is just my recommendation. Vary your holding size, your portfolio size and your knowledge in investing.

- Stick with stocks with a stock price over $2, an average daily volume of over 10,000 shares (8,000 for stock prices over $20) and a market cap over 200 million.

  Most big winners usually are in the price range of between $2 and $15 price and a market cap of between 200 million and 800 million. They represent the stocks that institutional investors are ignoring due to their restrictions. This is just a general guideline. Change them according to your requirements.

  I prefer to skip stocks of most emerging countries, especially the smaller companies as I do not trust their financial statements.

- Ignore the subscription services or books claiming that they make over 30% consistently. Some even have examples of making 5,000%. Most likely they tell you about the winners but not their losers.

  Check whether their portfolio uses cash or not. Most likely those portfolios that consistently make over 30% are not real.

  Alternatively they have 10 portfolios and they may only show you the one that makes a good profit. They could use the most favorable trades for the day for their virtual account. For example, the stock rose 20% late in the day and they claimed that they bought it on the open hour.

  When they back test their strategies, they can cheat on their performances with survivor bias (i.e. those bankrupted stocks are not in the historical database). If their returns are that great, do you think they really want share their secrets with a stranger like you?

Some made a big fortune and lost it all. So, the turtle investors who make small profits consistently win. Market timing and diversifying our portfolios help us winning consistently in the long run.

Besides screening dividend stocks yourself, there are many sites providing this information. You can google 'dividend stocks'. The following are some of them.

TopYields
http://www.topyields.nl/Top-dividend-yields-of-Dividend-Aristocrats.php

An ETF on Dividend Aristocrats
http://etfdb.com/index/sp-high-yield-dividend-aristocrats-index/

From Wikipedia on S&P Dividend Aristocrats
http://en.wikipedia.org/wiki/THE S&P_500_Dividend_Aristocrats

There are many sites to screen dividend stocks. I select Finviz.com as that should give us good result and it is free. In addition, we use the same site for market timing using SMA-20% and SMA-50%.

Screening is only the first step. You need to filter out the good stocks from the bad ones. When you have a handful of stocks, evaluate each one.

Link: Best dividend ETF:
https://www.youtube.com/watch?v=TPSw7On2gUo

Filler.
DRIP stands for dividend reinvestment plan. It uses the dividend to buy more stock of the company that pays the dividend automatically, and most likely with no commissions and some gives discounts of 2-3%.

- I have participated in these plans before. After a long while, the stocks bought from dividends were worth more than the initial stock prices. You need to keep track of the cost basis of the purchased stocks when you sell these stocks. Check out whether the company and/or your broker offer such programs. There are many sites that have more info of DRIPs such as Money Paper https://www.directinvesting.com/.

6 Rotate four ETFs

We can beat the market by rotating one ETF that represents the market such as SPY and cash via market timing. Aggressive investors can add SH or PSQ (contra ETFs) to the four to have better returns during market plunges.

During a market uptrend, rotating the following four ETFs could be more profitable than staying with SPY (or any ETF that simulating the market). Be warned that a short-term capital gain in taxable accounts is not treated as favorably as the long-term capital gain; check current tax laws.

The allocation percentages depend on your individual risk tolerance. You can use indexed mutual funds. Compare their expenses and restrictions. Some mutual funds charge you if you withdraw within a specific time period.

Select the best performer of last month (from Seeking Alpha, cnnFn, or one of many ETF/mutual fund sites). Add a contra ETF such as SH to take advantage of a falling market for more aggressive investors. Add sector ETFs to the described four ETFs such as XLY, XLP, XLE, XLF, XLU, IYW, XHB, IYM, OIL and XLU to expand your selection.

ETFs	Money Market	U.S.	International	Bond
Fidelity		Spartan Total Market	Spartan Global Market	Spartan US Bond
Vanguard		Total Stock Market	Total International Market	Total Bond Market
My choice	Fidelity	SPY	Vanguard	Fidelity
Suggest %				
During Market plunge	90%	0%	0%	10%
After plunge	10%	60%	20%	10%

Explanation

- The above are suggestions only. If your broker offers similar ETFs, consider using them.
- Check out any restrictions of the ETFs and commissions.

- 4 ETFs (one actually is a money market fund) are enough for most starters. They are diversified, low-cost and you do not need rebalancing except during a market plunge.
- The percentages are suggestions only. If you are less risk tolerant, allocate more to a money market fund, CD and/or bond ETF.
- Have at least 10% allocated to the money market fund for safety.
- When the market is risky, reduce stock equities (i.e. increase money market and bond allocations).
- The symbols for Fidelity ETFs are FSTMX, FSGDX and FBIDX.
- The symbols for Vanguard ETFs are VTSMX, VGTSX and VBMFX.
- If you are more advanced, use additional sector ETFs to rotate. Also buy long-term bond funds (such as 30-year Treasury) when the interest rates is 10% or more.

7 How to find the current best-performing sectors

There are many web sites that will show you the current best-performing sectors or ETFs for sectors. Depending on the web site, some may give you the best-performed ETFs for the last month or the last 30 days for example. If you rotate among a few sectors, you can maintain a record of their performance.

Seeking Alpha's home page has further divided the ETFs into the following groups: Sector, Industry (sub sector) and country. Pick the site you use most and/or your broker's site for this information.

Fidelity

Click on "News & Research" and then "Stock Market & Sector Performance" for sector performance and weighing recommendations. Fidelity offers the most choices for sector funds plus many sector commission-free ETFs. Most sector funds have penalties if you hold them less than 30 days (60 days for most sector funds in an annuity). Check the current restrictions.

8 SMA, MACD and Volume

Bring up Finviz.com. Enter SPY for your ticket symbol. The market trend is up if both SMA-20 and SMA-50 are positive. Finviz.com uses percent to indicate how far away the current price is above the average. The daily change of volume is also displayed. It is the confirmation indicator. When the price rises with low volume, it may not indicate the trend is up.

Use with MACD for better results. For simplicity, the trend is up when MACD is above the 0 line (usually in green color), and vice versa.

Most use daily charts (charting is not for beginners). Weekly charts should be used if the duration of holding the stock is longer. The above also applies for stocks trending down.

7 When to sell a stock

There are many reasons to sell a stock as follows.

Personal

1. Has met my targets/objectives.
   It could be a 10% gain in a very short-term swing, x% return in 4 months for a short-term swing or y% gain after a year for long-term trades. Define x and y depending on your risk tolerance and how often you trade.

   I bought 4 stocks in one day during the August, 2015 correction and placed sell orders with 10% more than my purchase prices. I sold one in a day and another one within a month. This is my strategy for correction – sometimes it works and sometimes it does not.

   Never look back. Do not blame yourself when the prices are better than your trade prices. When the market is volatile, use a higher percent of the current prices. Be disciplined. Stay on the same strategy and detach yourself from emotions.

2. Realize that we have made a mistake. Do not let your ego block your eyes. It could be due to bad analysis, bad, data, unexpected fraud, lawsuits, and/or unforeseeable events that you have no control of. It is better to get out with a small loss. I prefer a 25% loss as a threshold for long-term strategies and a 10% (or less for some strategies) loss for short-term strategies.

   We have to ensure whether it is a mistake or not. If the 'mistake' is just bad luck or due to conditions we cannot possibly predict or control, then it is not a mistake. If it is a mistake, learn from it. When we diversify, one bad loss should not cause a big dent in our portfolios. The stop loss is a good tool most of the time except when there is a flash crash.

   If the criteria have been faithfully followed and it does not work well, check out whether your criteria are wrong, or it does not work on the current market conditions.

3. When we have too many stocks in the same sector, we will want to replace some stocks to better diversify our portfolios.

When the sector is rising, we want to weigh more on that sector at the expense of diversification, and vice versa. Set a limit of how many sectors you should hold.

4. Need cash for living expenses.

5. To reduce a tax burden by selling some losers. Tax consideration should not be the primary reason for selling. Take advantage of the favorable tax treatment for long-term capital gains. In short, sell losers within the short term limit (currently a year), and sell winners after 365 days; check the current tax laws.

    Harvest tax losses. Sell losers and buy back similar stocks (or same stock after 31 days to avoid wash sale). It is not too clear in which you can buy back the same loser in your children's account under the current tax law.

6. To take advantage of a lower tax. In 2013, we can pay virtually zero (except the increase of tax on social security payment) Federal income taxes on long-term capital gains when our income is below a specific tax bracket (15% as of 2015). Check out the current tax laws. Evaluate the sold winners for a possible buy back.

Market Timing

7. When the market or the sector plunges, sell stocks or stocks within the sector.

    For temporary peaks, evaluate which stocks in your portfolio to sell based on fundamentals. The objective is to raise cash for buying opportunities.

Deteriorating appreciation potential

8. There may be some stocks that have a better appreciation potential than the ones you currently own. Churning the portfolio by replacing better stocks may cost some brokerage commissions (some are free today) and taxes for taxable accounts, but it improves the quality and the appreciation potential for the entire portfolio.

9. The company's fundamentals have changed for the worse. If you use a scoring system, compare the current score with the score you actually

bought the stock for. Apple is a good example from 2013 to 2015. Buy when the fundamentals are good and sell when they are not.

The basic fundamentals are expected P/E, the quarter-to-quarter earnings growth rate / the sales growth rate, and Debt /Equity.

When your stocks have passed the peak and started to decline, sell them. When they are heading to bankruptcy, sell them fast.

Hints that the fundamentals are degrading

Evaluate the stocks you own at least every 6 months and check their daily news at least once a week that can be easily done using Seeking Alpha's portfolio function.

- The cash flow is decreasing fast. Cash flow is not a particularly good predicative indicator for appreciation, but a good indicator on whether the company will survive. This metric is very hard to manipulate.

- A new or pending lawsuit. Check out how serious the lawsuit is and be aware that a minor lawsuit can be ignored. Companies always sue against each other.

- A big drop in sales. Do not be alarmed when a new product, or a new drug is going to replace a major product. Compare sales to the same quarter of prior year to avoid seasonal fluctuations (Q-to-Q info I available from Finviz.com).

- Management deteriorates- One hint is the deteriorating ROE from the last quarter.

- The extravagant life style of the CEO and the many easy loans to officers.

- Poor operations. They include recalls of products such as the GM recall on ignition switches, product secrets being stolen and customers' credit card info being stolen. Boeing's 747-Max is a warning call.

- A successful product from the competitor, or the current product is losing its market share, or becoming a low-profit commodity.

- Insiders and/or institutional investors are dumping the companies' stocks far more than the averages (2% for me) especially in heavy volumes and by more than one insider.

    - Have more than one insider dumping a lot of the stock within a month and no insider purchase in that month.

    - Have more than one insider decrease their holdings by more than 10%.

- When the SEC or any government agency pays attention to a company, it usually means bad news.

- Deceptive accounting practices have been discovered.

- Increasing receivable and/or inventory at an alarming rate.

- Earnings have been restated too many times.

- Short percentage is increasing fast – someone found something wrong with the company.

- The invalidity of 'one-time charges'.

- Abnormal return rate of the company's pension fund comparing to the average of the companies in the same sector.

- Too many and too costly reconstructing charges.

- The entire stock market is plunging as indicated by our chart in detecting market crashes.
- The stock price does not move up with good news. It shows the price has peaked.
- The accumulation amount is far less than the sold amount. When the stock price is up, the accumulation is less than the sold stocks when the stock price was down the last time. It indicates that no more accumulation is ahead and hence the stock will be down most likely.

Afterthoughts

- Another article on this topic.
  http://buzz.money.cnn.com/2013/04/05/stocks-sell/

An article from Investopedia. Nothing new but it is worth having the same second opinion.
http://www.investopedia.com/financial-edge/0412/5-tips-on-when-to-sell-your-stock.aspx

- It also depends on your strategies. I sell most of my stocks in my momentum portfolio within a month. At least one strategy I know of does not keep any stock during the peak stage of the market cycle – the easiest time to make money but also the riskiest time.

  If you use charts for trading, sell the stocks that are below your moving averages or other technical analysis indicators. Personally I do not use charts for making sell decisions due to my limited time.

- Sell when the company is heading into bankruptcy as described before. The red flags are: 1. Negative cash flow. 2. Heavy insiders dumping the stocks. 3. Pending major lawsuit. 4. Fraud from the management.

- Risky periods for a stock.
  Earnings announcement (4 times a year), settling a major lawsuit and/or during a FDA event in approving a drug are risky periods for a stock. A fluctuation more than 5% in either direction is normal. Some use options to buy insurance. Most ignore it. For the majority of the time, heavy insider purchase is a good indicator. There are rumors (or educated guesses) on earnings before their announcements. Zacks is supposed to be a good subscription for earnings estimates.

9 Selling a winner

Let the profit rise and at the same time protect your profit. Tesla quadrupled its value in 6 months. Examples abound such as Amazon and Yelp.

You do not want to sell these rocket stocks even if their fundamentals do not make sense. Buffett does not touch these stocks and he usually misses these big gains. However, many of these rocket stocks such as BRRY (Blackberry) will eventually fall losing most of their value. I bet the institutional investors move the market in either direction and usually they read the same analysts' reports. You profit as a contrarian if you have a good reason to act against the herd.

The following example uses a 10% trailing stop – mine is a little different from the official trailing stop described in the link section. Set the stop at 10% of the current price (i.e. 10% less than the current price), not the purchase price. You need to change the stop when the price rises but do not change it when the price falls. Review your stops every month or more frequently if time allows.

To illustrate, when the stock price rises to 100, set the stop at 90. When the stock price falls to 90, sell the stock at the market price. When the stock price rises to 200, change the stop at 180.

The stop should also be set according to how volatile the stock is. Some stocks are more volatile than others. Most charts show the resistance line. This line assumes the stock price should not fall below this line in normal fluctuations. Set the stop at 2% below this line so your stock will not be stopped out in theory.

To avoid flash crashes, do not place stop orders. Instead, do it mentally (mental stop is my term). When you see that the stock falls below your stop with no sign of a flash crash, sell the stock using a market order.

Of course, there is no bullet-proof scheme. This one should work in the long run. This is my suggestion only, so examine whether it works for you. Small cap and/or stocks with small average volumes fluctuate more.

Examples
I have too many bad examples of selling the stocks too early and sometimes holding them too long.

I made over 40% in a few weeks on ALU, but it went up more than 300% in the next two years. It was acquired in early 2016 by Nokia paying a good premium. I was right that ALU had a lot of valuable patents and I was wrong to dump it when I found out Cisco did not have any intention to acquire it – a big mistake by Cisco and the U.S.

FOSL is another example to teach us to use mental stop loss. FOSL was priced at $33.70 on 1/4/2010. Its fundamentals were just fine with an expected E/P (expected earnings yield) at 6% but decreasing earnings. It gained 115% later in 2010 - not expected.

On 1/3/2011, the expected E/P was still at around 6% and improving earnings. It gained 9% for the year – a little disappointing.

On 1/3/2012, the expected E/P was 7% and a huge earnings growth. Now, we expected a better performance for the year and it did by gaining 20%.

On 1/3/2013, the expected E/P was about 6% and the earnings gain was respectable. It gained 28% to $121. So far, so good.

On 1/2/2014, the E/P and the earnings growth were about the same as in 1/3/2013. However, it lost 7% for the year while SPY (an ETF simulating the market) gained 12%. There was no warning. Did the institutional investors lose the interest of this stock?

On 1/2/2015, the E/P was 7% and the earnings growth was about the same as the previous year. It lost 69% (vs. SPY's 0% return with dividends)!

From 1/4/2010 to 1/3/2016, the annualized return of FOSL is 0% (vs. SPY's 13%). Actually, after dividends, SPY should have an annualized return of about 15%. The lessons gained here are:

- Fundamentals (using EP and earnings growth in this example) may not always work. Otherwise, 2015 should have the same gain as 2014.
- The rosy outlook of the stock may be priced in already. When the outlook fails to materialize, the stock tanks.

Links: Fidelity Video: Trailing Stop Loss. 2 3
https://www.fidelity.com/learning-center/trading/trailing-stops-video
https://www.youtube.com/watch?v=l7EHWyOrfu4

https://www.investopedia.com/terms/t/trailingstop.asp

*** Bonus: Experiences

It has three sections: Performances from my book series "Best Stocks", my own experiences and the experiences from gurus with my own comments.

It has been hard to keep up all my trades and publish them in a book. Section #1 solves this problem as they are based on real recommendations.

Section #2 has my actual experiences past and present. Logically the present experiences do not have performances, and I may update them in the future.

Section #3 consists of articles and YouTube videos from Gurus..

Do not act without consulting your financial advisor first. The info could be obsolete by the time you read this book. I suggest the strategies and how we approach certain sectors and situations, and hopefully they will work. The market is not always rational, and hence first test out the strategy described and use stops to protect your portfolio.

#Fillers

Best complement. My late mother enjoyed Wheel of Fortune a lot, so are most folks. She did not even know English except the alphabets.

The only song I can sing in public is "Sound of Silence". If you understand my joke, sing it with me silently.

The $25 per hour wage can never compete with a $5 wage, same for $5 wage to a $1 wage. Moving factories to other countries such as S.E. Asia would increase pollution as most of these countries may not care about pollution.

We can do our part by not changing our mobile phones every year and live in smaller houses like apartments in China and many other countries.

Who is going to work with such generous welfare benefits and free money? This is why we have a supply-chain problem.

Section 1: Performance form "Best Stocks" series

1   Past Performances

Management Summary as of 7/01/21

The books in this series should be available on 7/15 and 12/15 in each year, but it is not a promise. I use the opening prices of 7/1/21 to update the performance info, so I can have more time to research stocks for this new book. Most are value stocks in the primary lists. The momentum stocks such as FAANG were doing very well in 2020, and SPY has more weights on these stocks; hence beating SPY is not easy in 2020.

This article "Past Performances" (not the rest of the book) can be freely distributed with mentioning the title of this book. This is for reference only, and I am not liable for any errors. The following performances are from my last three books in this series.

Book	Stocks	Return	Ann.	Beat SPY by[1]
Best Stocks for 2021 2nd Edition	10	20%	52%[3]	110%
Best Stocks for 2021	4	29%	52%	71%
Best Stocks to Buy from Aug, 2020	14	42%	45%	25%
Avg.	9	31%	50%	69%[2]

[1] See Methodology. "Beat SPY by" does not include commissions and dividends that would increase this ratio for winners.

[2] If you buy all stocks recommended in the primary lists (secondary lists are also described separately), you should have an annualized returns of 50% and beat SPY (representing the market) by about 69% without considering dividends and fees. If this average is less than 2%, do not buy the book until it will work again; I need to change my strategies to meet the current market conditions.

[3] CTB selected in "Best Stocks for 2021 2nd Edition" has been delisted (most likely has been acquired). It is my better winner (it returned 44% and 217% annualized on 4/22/2021), and hence the return of the portfolio should be better than the stated.

You buy this book or similar books because you expect the selected stocks are profitable. A 1,000+ page book with a poor performance record would cost you money. Even a one-page book will make you money if the recommended stocks perform, as you are paying for the exhaustive research behind the selection.

No one can predict the future performance of his or her selected stocks. Based on the last year of the books in this series, the chance of success of my selection is good for this book. If it continues to work, the price of the book is peanuts. If it does not, it would be harmful even if it is free.

I have many strategies (same as screens) and I usually choose those strategies that work well recently. The screened stocks will be compared to my own criteria with some exceptions. Hence, most are value stocks that should be better positioned to a down market. I do attempt to time the market as described in this book. I bought many of the stocks I recommended. Some buy orders have not been executed as they had risen too fast at the gate.

There are many vendors recommending stocks and showing their 'fantastic' results that they selected their favorable periods, or trading with the best prices of the day. Some showed you the returns of the big winners, but not the big losers. I will show you the performances of my last 3 books. Past performances have nothing to do with future performances. Refer to Disclaimer under Introduction.

The rest of the article describes the performances of the stocks in more detail on the last three books in this series. Each book has a primary list and any sub lists.

Book #1: "Best Stocks for 2021 2nd Edition"
Start date: 02/08/2021. End date: 07/01/2021.
CTB has been delisted as of 7/1/2021. The price on the recommended date is $35 and the price on 6/17/2021 is 40.12, and it is my best winner in this group. From my last update on 4/24/2021, it returned 44% and 217% annualized.

Symbol	Return	Annualized
BG	5%	14%
CBNK	40%	103%
CTB	N/A	N/A
CUBI	49%	126%
HMST	-1%	-1%
JEF	28%	72%
MLI	14%	36%
OPY	34%	88%
TPVG	6%	15%
UVSP	5%	13%
Average	20%	52%
SPY	10%	25%
Beat SPY by	110%	

Short-term lists

There are two bonus lists: Momentum and Short. These lists are short-term, and hence I use one month as the end dates.

Start date: 02/08/2021. End date: 03/10/2021.

Momentum (7 stocks)

Symbol	Return	Ann.
ATGE	-6%	-68%
ATRS	-11%	-134%
CMRE	15%	182%
REGI	-26%	-318%
RIO	0%	-1%
SPWH	0%	-1%
WIRE	8%	96%
Average	-3%	-35%
SPY	0%	-3%
Beat SPY by	-1100%	

Short selling betting the stocks to go down (3 stocks).

Symbol	Return	Ann.
HYLN	16%	191%
NEXT	2%	332%
RMO	40%	482%
Average	28%	335%
SPY	0%	-3%
Beat SPY by	11,571%	

Since SPY's return is close to zero, the "Best SPY by" has no meaning. This momentum list does not perform, but the short list does.

The short-term lists may not be provided in future books, as they are too volatile and have little value to readers due to time span from the initial publish date.

Book #2: "Best Stocks for 2021"

Start Date: 12/10/2020. End Date: 07/01/2021.

Besides the primary list of recommended stocks, I have several other lists. Year-End lists are short-term, and the End Date is 01/10/2021. I provide 2nd month and 3rd month holding to determine what is a better holding period for the current selection.

Summary:

List (# of stocks)	Return	Annualized	Beat SPY
Primary list (4)	29%	52%	71%
Primary list without GLD (3)	39%	71%	135%
Secondary list (6)	46%	84%	177%
Year-End list (5)	5%		68%
Secondary list for Year-End (5)	-1%		-125%
Secondary list without foreign countries (2)	14%		342%[1]

Details

1. Primary list.

Primary List (stocks = 4)	Return	Annualized	Beat SPY
DSK	84%	151%	
ESGR	20%	35%	
GLD	-4%	-7%	
OTTR	15%	27%	
Average	29%	52%	71%
SPY	14%		

2. Primary list without GLD.

Primary List (stocks = 3)	Return	Annualized	Beat SPY
DSK	84%	151%	

ESGR	20%	35%	
OTTR	15%	27%	
Average	39%	71%	135%
SPY	17%		

GLD is a hedge for inflation, and it should not be included in the primary list, but I did.

3. Secondary list.

Secondary List (stocks = 5)	Return	Annualized	Beat SPY
BCC	46%	126%	
GPI	35%	95%	
HEAR	43%	118%	
HVT	53%	144%	
HZO	75%	204%	
Average	46%	84%	177%
SPY	17%	30%	

Most of the stock selected in this list have high dumping by the insiders. It seems the insiders were wrong and they are usually not wrong.

4. Year-End Loser list.

From 12/10/2020 to 1/10/2021. Include the performances keeping this portfolio for 2 and 3 months. This is the official list for year-end losers. There are other options and they will be used for future selections.

Year-End (5 stocks)	Return	Ann %	Beat SPY	Beat SPY
Hold period	1 Month	1 Month	2 Months	3 Months
BCOR	20%	224%	28%	26%
CEPU	-10%	-114%	-10%	-17%
EEX	-8%	-94%	-3%	30%
GANG	17%	191%	38%	62%
STFC	9%	105%	1%	22%

Average	5%	63%	11%	25%
SPY	3%	37%	6%	6%
Beat SPY	68%		70%	298%

The above result suggests us to hold the stocks for 3 months instead of 1. It could be due to the better performance of GANG from 17% to 62%. SPY has a lot of growth stocks and they suffer from a dip during the third month.

4A. Year-End Loser Secondary list

Year-End (5 stocks)	Return	Ann %	Beat SPY	Beat SPY
Hold period	1 Month	1 Month	2 Months	3 Months
ADES	-4%	-47%	3%	3%
BMA	-17%	-190%	-14%	-18%
DXC	14%	163%	3%	17%
PAM	-12%	-140%	-5%	-3%
PLCE	15%	166%	68%	71%
Average	-1%		12%	14%
SPY	3%		6%	6%
Beat SPY	-125%		87%	124%

The foreign stocks do not perform, but the performance has improved immensely for holding 3 months.

4B. Year-End Loser Secondary list with US companies only.

Year-End (2 stocks)	Return	Ann %	Beat SPY	Beat SPY
Hold period	1 Month	1 Month	2 Months	3 Months
DXC	14%	163%	3%	17%
PLCE	15%	166%	68%	71%
Average	14%	164%	36%	44%
SPY	3%		6%	6%

Beat SPY	342%		464%	605%

This list turns out to have the best performance of the 3 year-end lists.

Book #3: "Best Stocks to buy from August, 2020"

The performance is the returns from 07/28/2020 to 07/01/2021 (close to the next book in the series). The average of the 14 recommended stocks beats SPY (an ETF simulating S&P 500 stocks) by 29%. **The 25% is unbelievable** as SPY has been weighed heavily with a lot of tech stocks such as Apple, Tesla and Microsoft, and they had been increased in value substantially during this period. If you believe they will continue this trend, SPY or any ETF weighed on tech stocks would be beneficial. However, I believe they are peaking and the fall seems inevitable – it is my personal opinion. All 14 selected stocks are winners. Again, dividends and fees have not been included. CMCSA and FDX are big winners profiting from the pandemic. True EY is obtained at the time of evaluation, about a year ago.

Symbol	Sector	True EY	Return 07/01/21	Ann. Return
ABBV	Drug	7%	16%	18%
ABT	Drug	3%	16%	17%
CHE	Diversified	4%	4%	5%
CMCSA	Media	11%	32%	35%
FDX	Transport	8%	79%	85%
GTS	Health	N/A	15%	16%
JNJ	Drug	6%	12%	13%
MCK	Drug	8%	24%	26%
MSFT	Software	4%	34%	37%
SCHN	Metal	10%	163%	177%
SMCI	Computer	11%	25%	27%
UFPI	Building	10%	32%	34%
UNH	Health	9%	34%	36%
ZBRA	Computer	5%	95%	103%
Avg.			42%	45%
		SPY	33%	36%
	Beat SPY			25%

At one time UFPI was a loser.

Methodology

- 'Beat SPY by "= (Return − SPY's return) / (SPY's return) with adjustments to negative numbers.
- Dividends and fees are not included. Hence, the ratio usually looks better than it actually is.

-
- Past performances have nothing to do with future performances.
  So far, the last two books have performed well with the market conditions.

  The performances are for reference only. These incredible performances are not sustainable. **Consult your financial advisor** before taking any action. The author and the publisher are not liable for any errors.
-
- Start date usually is the publish date, and end date usually is the publish date of the next book in the series. May add the performance for one year. Dates could be one or two days off due to non-trading days.
-
- Short-term trades such as Year-End strategy is usually one month duration. May add 2-month and 3-month durations for comparison.
- True EY is the earnings yield considering debts and cash. Compare it to one-year Treasuries and CDs which are basically risk free. It is the reciprocal of "EV/EBITDA". It is obtained from Yahoo!Finance (under Statistics).
-
- Most figures are rounded up for easy reading, but not in the calculation in "Beat SPY by".
-
- Once in a while, the performance is not correct due to many uncontrolled events such as delisting a stock (due to bankruptcy, merger...).
-
- There are older books. However, I cannot get the performances due to the survival bias (i.e. the delisted stocks are no longer in the database).

Section 2: My experiences

1 Beginners' major mistakes

There are plenty and some have been described in this book. The following is my summary.

- If your strategy is targeted for long term trading, keep the acquired stocks for a year or longer. If it is short term, keep the stocks less than 3 months (there are many exceptions). In any case, sell the acquired stock when the loss is over your limit. My limit is 20% for volatile stocks and 15% for non-volatile stocks. If Finviz's beta for the stock is more than 1.2, more likely it is non-volatile and 0.8 or less for volatile stocks. If the beta is negative, it indicates the stock price fluctuates opposite to the market.

- It is hard to beat the professionals in short-term trading and day trading. Hence, concentrate in long-term trading. Start with ETFs.

- Let the profit rise. If you want to protect your profit, use trailing stops. I made 200% on GameStop in 2021. If I let the profit rise, I should at least make another 200%.

- Do not act according to tips / news / secrets. By the time it reaches you, it would be too late. There are exceptions such as reliable sources from insiders (it could violate security laws). I acted a little late in selecting a stock from many companies producing vaccines for this pandemic, but I still made good money.

- Do not trust the government but do not fight against the city hall. When they print money to save the market, buy commodities for example. When our government tried to delist Chinese stocks, we should sell most of them.

- Do not put all eggs in the same basket (i.e. you should diversify your investment). I made a mistake in 2020 betting the market would fall due to the economy and many opinions from gurus. In the first half of 2021, the market has been making new highs. Luckily I did not lose a lot and I was saved by another small account making about 100% due to luck in owning Game Stop stocks.

- Be emotionally detached from your investment. It is only money and not your life. This book helps you reduce risk in investing.

- Learn from our mistakes, and move on. I have repeated so many mistakes that I need to read my book again and again.

- The lessons from many billionaires may not apply to you. Many had lost almost all of the money at one time. I prefer making money slowly and consistently as described in this book.

- Concentrate on U.S. companies. Many foreign countries do not have organizations similar to our SEC, and politics, insider trading and fraud could affect their stock prices. Unless you are experts in the country, buy ETFs for the country that you expect favorable.

- Avoid buying a stock before its earnings report date (available from Finviz). The favorable news would have been priced in already. Very seldom, the positive surprise is better than the expected; in this case you can make good money.

- We all made mistakes and missed opportunities, and we will continue to do so. I missed acquiring Tesla for example and I betted the market would go down in 2021 (the printing money saved the market). Now I believe technical is better than fundamentals in market timing. Learn from the mistakes and move on.

- When you are successful, help the poor and the unprivileged. We can use so much money in our lives.

2   Super long-term investing

I am more a value investor than a growth investor. The difference between the two is keeping the stock longer for value investing (a year to me). A growth investor weighs the momentum metrics (such as SMA) more than fundamentals. A growth investor would rotate stocks and/or sectors more frequently (one to three months to me).

Usually I sell my value stocks after they satisfy my objectives, and the holding period is about a year. I seldom have stocks appreciated more than 100%. Some did more than 100% due to many factors such as not reviewing my portfolio early enough, holding them less than 1 year in my taxable accounts or being merged.

Recently, I discovered my TTWO has appreciated 6 times in the last 6 years from May, 2015 representing 100% appreciation per year. It proves 'never sold' is a good strategy too, if there is a good reason. The reason for this stock is gaming would be big for our generation, and it is very hard and expensive for newcomers into games.

The fundamentals of TTWO were not fantastic in 2015, and that was the reason I bought it so cheap. Many analysts thought the stock would not perform after its franchise game. If there is a good reason, contrary investing could be profitable.

This stock is in a gift account and I do not want to place a stop order. I am sure it would be stopped out using trailing stops. If I need to use trailing stops on this stock, I would use 20% on the current price and review the stop periodically (say monthly).

I should use the same strategy in many of my value stocks, and I hope to report more of them in the future. That is the reason why some investors are very profitable, even their portfolios lose more than 50%. We should let the winners rise and the losers out.

3 Vaccines and the investor

You cannot use fundamentals to analyze vaccine stocks. It depends more on whether the vaccines are required every year and any serious side effects.

- I did not invest in vaccines initially for the following reason. SARS disappeared for no reason. Many companies lost money in SARS vaccines and the cures.

- I invested small amounts instead of a large one on Moderna due to high dumping from the insiders. I keep betting on their technique that could fix other diseases and the booster shots. As of 8/2021, they are doing well. One bought in 4/1/21, returned 40% and another one bought in 5/1/2021, returned 300%. From these results, the insiders so far were wrong and the entry points make a big difference. The third shot and the chance of needing a shot every year could boost the stock price further. It covered many of the stock losses due to stopping out.
- I missed J&J due to the lawsuits on baby powders. It could be the ideal vaccine with low temperature to store and it is only a one-shot deal. However, they discovered a minor side effect recently. The stock has been doing great.
- Pfizer's vaccines may not make them big money: it is a big company to start with and the technology is not theirs. They just involve manufacturing and distribution.
- China's vaccine companies do not make a lot of profits and their stocks stay level. It is due to China giving most of the vaccines free. In addition, we have to be careful in the US delisting Chinese stocks.
- Nexalis is a big winner. I should have spotted it via screens. I did not, and hence I am a loser on this.

Performances from 1/3/2021 to 11/1/2021 (today)

	Return	Annualized
Moderna	154%	185%
J&J	5%	6%
Pfizer	19%	23%
SPY	27%	33%

4   Lessons from my trading in 2019-2020

2020 is a miserable year with the pandemic, but reasonably well for the market. Again, I am too conservative and have not followed by my own advice illustrated in my books. If you followed my SMA-350 (Simple Moving Average for the last 350 sessions), you should have done amazingly well. Technical chart (SMA in my case) worked far better than the fundamentals in 2020. Tesla made about 6 times even the P/E was over 1,000 at one time in 2020.

I made many financial mistakes along with some good decisions in 2019. I have explained how to avoid some mistakes in my books and I did not follow my own preaching.

In the last two months of 2019, I started buying contra ETFs betting the market would go down while the market has been making new highs. The market is financially unsound but technically sound. Lesson #1: Follow the simplest market timing described in this book. Lesson #2: Never bet against the market in the year before the election.

There are always two sides on the opposite views of the market. I studied them and believe 2020 could be a disastrous year for the market. No one is sure unless s/he has a time machine. Again follow Lesson #1.

I did well in buying GLD/SLV (currently SLV is doing better than GLD), and basic materials including IYW and two copper miners. I will unload some copper miners. Lesson #3: Every portfolio should have a small portion in gold (GLD/or similar ETFs, gold coins and an ETF for gold miners).

Stay away from Chinese stocks for the entire year. I may buy a contra ETF on Chinese stocks. The trade war, delisting and the explosive debts will drive China's economy down for a few years.

I had 50% profit in one month using my year-end strategy in 2018. From my memory, I made about 100% on YRCW and lost about 30% on another buy on the same stock. Lesson #4: "Year-End Strategy" works at least so far. Lesson #5: Sell the stocks bought using this strategy within 2 months, and hence I should use retirement accounts for this strategy.

I made some money in trading energy stocks that have been beaten down badly. The outlook of energy stocks is not good. Lesson #6: Buy low and sell high. Lesson #7: Buffett's "Be greedy when everyone is fearful and vice versa" is correct thinking.

There are many 'great' traders making millions and losing most. Lesson #8: Avoid big losses by using stops. Lesson #9: Do not speculate and be a turtle investor.

Sold METC and REI in early 2020 for 14% gain (172% annualized) and 35% (508%) respectively. They were screened from my year-end strategy in early Dec., 2019 and profited due to the daily news (Iran). Lesson #10: Combine different strategies.

I have saved the most important lesson for last. If you spend all day long trading, you will not enjoy life and it is bad for your physical health and mental health. Wish you a healthy and prosperous 2021!

#Fillers:

How messed up our welfare system is?

It encourages our citizens to be lazy and let the government bail them out. It encourages more children and teenage mothers.

Do you take a job when you lose all the goodies and free health care?

Many take care of their old parents and get paid handsomely.
One divorced his wife to boost the SSI, and then married a foreigner lady who gave him $30,000 plus free sex.

One of the best sellers in Taiwan is "How to retire comfortably with no work".

The middle class is being squeezed by the rich (who do not pay much taxes) and the poor.

#Filler: Ghosts

I have proved there are no ghosts. If they were, the Chinese ghost and the American ghost should act and look the same.

#Filler: Communism to capitalism

China and Vietnam changed from communism to capitalism in recent history. They are both prosperous. Cuba and N. Korea stick to communism, and are still poor. India has been capitalists for a long while, and is still poor. The governance is more important than the type of government in most cases.

5   Lessons from selling GME

Game Stop (symbol GME) has been up 16 times from the low and still is climbing up as of this writing. There are several lessons to learn and review.

- Super stocks. Based on your time available for monitoring stocks, you should have a handful of stocks comprised the majority of your portfolio; I have about 10. GME and GILD were my super stocks at one time. Both were more than 3 times my average position.

- Stops. Both GME and GILD were in the downward trend when they were acquired. I was glad I did not use stops on them to give the market more time to recognize their real values. I sold GILD before the surge. Lesson: Do not put stops on value stocks, but it is fine on momentum and/or on short selling. With manual stops, you may lose up to 100% at most, but not 1,600% in the worst case for GME.

- Shorting. Do not short stocks when the short percent (from Finviz or other sources) is over 20%; usually I use 10%.

- Short squeeze. GME had experienced serious a short squeeze. The trade volume for one day was 140M, while the number of floating shares was only 50M. Lesson: Watch out for the short percent. The stocks that have short percentage over 25% (from Finviz) are buy candidates.

- I do not understand why the short shares can be more than the floating shares (114%). Some shares could be shorted more than one time.

- I sold 1/3 at about $26 and the majority at about $40 just a few days later. I should follow my article on selling winners.

- Usually I keep a good record of the stocks I bought. I did not this time. Hence, I cannot tell you my real returns and my annualized returns and the comparisons to S&P 500. Most stock brokers do not give you the buy date. You need to include the metrics such as P/E and Debt/Equity for future evaluation of other stocks. A simple spreadsheet will do the housekeeping. From my estimate, I made about 300% in trading GME.

- I will not buy it back for several reasons: (1) It has more than its fair value (still losing money), (2) The short squeeze will be over if not already, (3) Most malls have few visitors as this writing, (4) The future of buying software is via downloading, (5) They do not have moats and advantage over their competitors such as Amazon and Target, and (6) The management is good in selling pet food, which is quite different from selling video games and consoles. Do not look back. As of 2/4/2021, it went up to more than 400 and today's price is 92.

- From Finviz, I read 2 good articles on GME.

- Luck has a lot to do with this trade. If I waited for a week, my profit could be many times. Usually I sold my stocks after making 100%, not I made 300%. A broker offered cash for moving to their account. I did not look at this account where I have my GME more often than my primary account.

- It is a crazy situation that retail investors are giving the hedge funds and their investors a tough time; some may go bankrupt and their investors would lose a lot. Invest in hedge funds carefully. Hedge funds used to take advantage of retail investors. They lead us to trade what they want us to trade and determine the trends of many stocks. With social media, the retail buyers strike back.

#Filler: Are you politically correct?

"All lives matter".

"The black commit more crimes".

"There are fewer women in science and technology fields".

All the above are incorrect politically, even if they are facts. Some have lost their jobs for speaking out. Our society does not allow us to speak of the problems. If we do not know our problems, how can we fix them?

#Filler: Freedom of wearing masks?

We should if it does not affect others. With the hospitals fully used, should those patients who wear masks have higher priority?

6   Disasters in 2020 and 2021?

2021 is not a good year according to Chinese astronomy. The curse of Tippecanoe has materialized from 1840 to 1960: The presidents who were elected in the years that are evenly divided by 20 died.

There are some predictions that the U.S. will suffer a lot in 2020. Some predictions are correct and some including the "world end in 2012" are not. Hence, this article should belong to the Conspiracy Theories. Even with some good arguments, I am **not totally convinced**. However, I would take actions, similar to buying insurance. I would like to invest in gold and foreign countries (but all countries will be on fire if the prediction is correct). I will limit my Chinese stock holdings in 2020 for sure.

Prediction #1 (materialized as of 2/2020). To some, China has a cycle of disasters every 60 years and 2020 is supposed to be the year for disasters. It happened in the last three: 1960 Great Famine (1959-1961 estimated 30 million died), 1900 Boxer Rebellion (1899 – 1901) and 1840 First Opium War (1839 – 1842). I cannot find any major disaster in 1780 and the Sino-Japan War was not in the cycle year. It has 3 rights and 2 wrongs – not a bad bet.

Prediction #2. Some predictors believe that the USD would lose the reserve currency status. It is quite possible as we have been printing too much USD and our national debt is ridiculously high compared to our GDP. The hint today is that some countries are not using the USD for trading. The "One Belt, One Road" is another example, where the participants are trading with Chinese and /or Russian currencies.

Secondly, they also believe there will be an overdue earthquake that would destroy California. Despite any predictions, it would happen but hopefully not in my lifetime. It could destroy Silicon Valley and Hollywood, the most important areas for our economy. The stock market could lose most of its value. The Federal government would not likely be able to rescue California on this scale and that could lead California to become independent. It is likely but I do not bet on it. Luckily, this prediction does not happen in 2020.

The two events if materialized would possibly cause a global depression and even civil wars. Election year is traditionally a good year for the market, but we should be cautious with our money this time.

Believe it or not? Another conspiracy theory? But, do not say you were not warned. Personally I do **not** believe it**,** but I will take some actions just like buying insurance. I hope the predictions are wrong. For more info, check out Billy Meier from the web. He did have some correct predictions but some of his photos were falsified.

It could be the most entertaining article in this book, or the most important one. Even if there is no disaster, it is always better to diversify with gold (about 10% I suggest) and to sell short when the market is risky.

https://www.thebalance.com/dollar-collapse-how-to-protect-yourself-and-survive-3306263
Written on 8/2019.

Update 1/2020.
\# There are plagues in years ending with '20' such as 1720, 1820, 1920 and this year 2020. We did have locust attacks in E. Africa and India in 2020. Is it a coincidence?

Update 3/2020.
\# The virus spreads to Europe and the U.S. It could cause a global depression.

\# U.S. tries to solve the financial crisis by excessively printing money. It could cause inflation and the USD will be shaken (Prediction #2). So far, China seems to recover from the virus, and it adds fire to our USD. We protect our USD via policy, military power and trust. The trust part is losing.

Prediction #3, as of 4/2020
If U.S. asks China for damages, China would likely refuse. If the debt of about 1.07 T is frozen, China would take counter action. This would lead to military war and WW3. Even if it does not happen, consider decoupling. Despite all these actions against China, I have a small investment on FXI and bet it will be fine long term.

Prediction #4, as of 10/2020.
So far all presidents elected in the same year as the disaster cycle (60 years apart as 庚子年) died: William Henry Harrison (elected on 1841, missed by 1 year I guess), William McKinley (1900) and Kennedy (1960). Coincident? In astronomy, it occurs when some planets lie in a straight line.

With the old age of our presidential candidates elected in 2020 [Update. Biden was elected], the chance is quite high this year. Biden's VP candidate has very good signs in Chinese astronomy (I am more a scientist but I cannot ignore it with so many predictions that have been materialized. I bet she will be the first female president within 5 years even it may not be widely accepted in our lifetime.

7 How to prepare for disasters

This article prepares you for some of the predicted disasters in 2020, which may never materialize. [Update 03/2020. Pandemic has happened and the breakout was in China.] However, it also helps you to prepare yourself for any future disasters. The disasters may never happen but your actions are the insurance for protecting yourself. Depending on your risk tolerance, allocate 2% to 10% for this effort. I divide the actions into several categories as follows. As to all my recommendations, you should consult your financial advisor before taking any actions, especially the risky ones like this one.

Preparing for the depreciation of the USD (U.S. Dollar)

As of 5/2020, this has not happened, and I hope it will not happen in my lifetime. The government has been printing too much USD and the economy may not be that rosy as our government has described as of 2019. As a result, the USD could lose the reserve currency status. We know what happened to the U.K. when the pound was replaced by USD. In preparing for a market plunge, we usually accumulate cash, and / or buy safe Treasury Bills. It may not work this time as USD could lose its buying power.

Here are my suggestions on what to buy. Buy gold (GLD, IAU for ETFs, RING for gold miner and gold coins), and silver (SLV for ETF and silver coins). Despite the delisting, I invest in FXI, an ETF for Chinese companies. I bet Yuan, the Chinese currency would appreciate. Most investors should have 5% to 20% in gold investment.

When we have detected a market plunge via market timing, buy contra ETFs for risky investors.

Talk to your financial advisor before taking any actions. I am **not responsible** for your loss or gain. As of 2019, it is too early to prepare for this disaster.

Protecting your lives

Protect yourself from a stage of no government and police protection.

Action
Buy guns or weapons (I'm for gun control with a realistic approach).
Store enough food.
Store enough water.
Store enough wood.
Store enough gasoline and have a generator.

8 Airlines

I have to repeat it again: All my articles are my approach on selecting stocks. Do not invest without consulting your financial advisor. As of this writing where all the metrics and prices are based on today (8/10/2021), I do not know the future performances of my recommended stocks and most authors including myself present the recommended stocks after the fact whether they are successful or not. In this case, learn from my approach, and you can repeat them if it is proven to be profitable.

I believe the jet manufacturers will have a long time to recover. Boeing could be bailed out by the U.S. government for national security and jobs. Hopefully the U.S. airlines will recover next year (2022), provided the pandemic is subdued.

If you do not have time to evaluate airlines and you bet the airline industry would recover, JETS, an ETF for airlines, is a good choice. As in almost all investments, timing is the key. In this example, JETS has a recent low of around $12 in May, 2020 and a recent high of $28 in March, 2021. You may ask why I did not buy on the low and sell at the high. My answer is that I do not have a time machine. Today's (as of 8/2021) it is around $23, not far from the recent high, but far away from the high of $32 in Jan., 2020. Compared to other sectors, the price is low. We bet the airline sector will turn around. I am looking for an entry point at $15.

The following metrics (preferred by me) of several airlines are used for comparison. Most metrics are obtained from Finviz, Yahoo!Finance, Fidelity or my estimate on 8/10/2021. I am not responsible for any errors.

Airline	American	Delta	Southwest	United	JetBlue
Debt /Eq	N/A[1]	22.7	1.2	7.1	1.2
Quick ratio	1.0	0.8	1.5	1.3	1.0
Sales Q/Q	362%	384%	298%	271%	598%
Earnings Q/Q	101%	113%	135%	80%	117%
Forward P/E	23	9	16	12	14
True yield[2]	-13%	-16%	-2%	-16%	-10%
Fidelity's ESS[3]	4	5	2	5	3
Insider Tran.	0%	-2%	-10%	-4%	-5%

[1] Most likely, the Equity is negative and hence it is not available.

[2] It is the reversal of Enterprise Value/EBITDA (from Yahoo!Finance).
[1] Equity Summary Score from 0 to 10 (10 is the best). All airlines score low.

I would skip American and Delta due to the high Debt / Eq. United at 7.1 is not too promising.

Southwest and JetBlue score high for me. However, they score low by Fidelity and their own insiders.

Forward P/E is an estimate and is based on future earnings, the lower the better. True Yield is based on past earnings.

The above research plus the writing is done in less than two hours, but I have a lot of recent thoughts on this sector. I just gathered the info and researches by other folks. Due to the time limit, I have not checked out the outlook of each company (Yahoo!Finance is one source and Finviz.com is another among many).

Filler   Afghan.

- We cannot solve all the world's problems and conflicts. The U.S. would be in better financial shape without the Vietnam War and the Afghan. War. We are glad the war has finally ended.

  Similar to the Vietnam War, we never learn from the Brits and Russians. That is why Afghan. was called "the cemetery of empires".

- We cannot win the war even with our advanced weapons and jets as most areas are hilly and their fighters are dedicated. Why are we so war-addictive besides taking care of our 'defense' companies?

- Just like Saigon, the Afghan government is very corrupt. The U.S. should investigate **our folks in this corruption.**

On the lighter side, they could load at least 10 persons more in the C-19 by allowing children and females in first and disallowing folks over 200 pounds. For saving at least 10 lives per trip, I should have won a Nobel Prize, and I am more deserved than Obama for doing nothing.

9   Value or Momentum?

When the market favors value, buy an ETF on value stocks, and vice versa. You can determine the trend of the corresponding ETF via SMA-10 and SMA-50 from Finviz.

The following is my test results using EY, Expected Earnings Yield (Price/Expecting Earnings) and a Timing Rank provided by a vendor. EY is a primary value matric.

The data could be a little off and they are used for illustration purposes. I am not responsible for any errors.

I included the stocks in the three major exchanges only. I had 4 tests in 1 year for 2 years. I selected the top 10 stocks or less if not available and got the return after one year (usually a few days off). RSP (an evenly weighted ETF for the S&P 500 stocks) is used as a yardstick.

	EP	Timing Rank	RSP
01/03/2019	58%	2%	29%
04/01/2019	120%	-40%	-24%
07/01/2019	-49%	7%	-6%
10/01/2019	-26%	14%	2%
01/03/2020	-9%	152%	9%
04/01/2020	540%	71%	79%
07/01/2020	388%	83%	49%
10/01/2020	186%	7%	40%
Average	151%	37%	22%

Comments.

- The market has been great for these two years. It is obviously a bull market. Performances are better by selecting stocks (active management) than buying the entire S&P 500 stocks.
- Value investing is better than Momentum investing during the test periods.
- I double checked on the incredible 540% and 186% returns and I did not find any error.

I also find the percentages of losers, maximum and minimum values for both EP and Timing Rank (not listed here).

10   When to close the shorts

As described, you can close the shorts periodically (say monthly) and/or the loss reaches a specific amount (I use 20% and 25% for volatile stocks).

When the market has a temporary down (such as more than 1% loss in this rising market in 2021), I close all my shorts.

The following is what I did on 09/29/2021.

Stocks	Short Date	Close date	Duration	Return	Annualized
ACVA	06/10/21	09/29/21	111	22%	72%
CCL	07/14/21	09/29/21	77	-8%	-36%
CENX	09/17/21	09/29/21	12	3%	105%
CLOV	09/16/21	09/29/21	13	10%	291%
CSPR	09/16/21	09/29/21	13	33%	917%
EOSE	09/15/21	09/29/21	14	10%	261%
MILE	07/22/21	09/29/21	69	53%	279%
NCLH	07/27/21	09/29/21	64	-5%	-27%
REAL	06/04/21	09/29/21	117	22%	68%
UAVS	06/04/21	09/29/21	117	41%	127%
Average	07/30/21	09/29/21	61	18%	206%
RSP				0%	-1%

Comments and explanations.
- It is for education purposes and I am not responsible for any errors. As in most parts of this book, commissions, dividends and fees (interest for shorts) are not included, and hence the returns are less than specified. They are real trades for the period.
- When I have more than one trade on the same stock, I use the price of the one with the largest quantity.
- Two small losers and 8 winners. The average return is 18% for an average of a holding period of 61 days, and is quite good especially in the rising market in 2021. I usually recommend shorting stocks in a falling market.
- The annualized returns have been exaggerated for durations less than 30 days.
- "Short date" is the same as "Sell date", while "Close date" is the same as "Buy date". As in shorting, you sell before you buy.

- I recommend closing the short positions after a holding period of 30 days unless you have reasons to hold the shorts longer. In this case, holding two months is optimal.
- I closed all positions on 09/29/21 and I could have higher profits by lowering the close prices.
- RSP is used as a yardstick. It is similar to SPY, an ETF consisting of S&P 500 stocks. RSP is a better yardstick than SPY, as it is weighed evenly. In this period, the market is flat.

I did the same on 11/17/21 and used 97% of the current prices to close (buy) the short positions.

Stocks	Short Date	Close date	Duration	Return	Annualized
BBIG[1]	09/30/21	11/19/21[1]	50	35%	258%
BFLY	09/30/21	11/18/21	49	14%	107%
EOLS	11/10/21	11/17/21	7	10%	523%
FLDM	10/13/21	11/18/21	36	14%	147%
MKFG	10/27/21	11/18/21	22	-9%	-149%
PAVM[1]	10/20/21	11/19/21[1]	30	34%	413%
TSP	10/05/21	11/18/21	44	-11%	-91%
VRM	10/13/21	11/17/21	35	13%	135%
Average	10/14/21	11/18/21	34	13%	168%
RSP				4%	294%

[1] As of this writing during the early morning of 11/19/21, these two stocks have not been closed and I used the morning prices and 11/19/21 as the Close Date. Will try to close these two positions later today.

All the comments / explanations of the first table still hold. Here are the comments specific to the above table.
- Due to the market and the lower close prices, I only closed two positions on the first day, 4 on the second day and still 2 unclosed on the third day.
- There are two losers and six winners.

The "Annualized Return" has been distorted. I prefer to stick with "Return", and 13% Return is quite good, especially RSP (representing the market) is up by 4% in the same period.

11 Miscellaneous

Due to the production cost and the expanding size of this book, this section can be accessed from the [web](#) only.

https://ebmyth.blogspot.com/2021/02/book-3-section-iv-experiences.html

#Filler

Someone is right in using bleach to cure the virus. When the guy dies, his virus dies also. LOL.

#Filler: Nothing perfect

If we have no wars and no pandemic for the last 2,000 years, the population would explode.

If we have no sinners, heaven would be full by now.

#Filler: Coward to gift

An old lady ordered just a bowl of white rice. I should have ordered some meat for her. I was afraid of being admired as a 'good' guy and/or hurting her feelings. Will not happen again!

I left my table to pick up a drink in a fast-food place. A guy tried to eat my lunch.

We are one of the richest countries. How could these incidents happen?

Section 3: Gurus' experiences

It has three sections: Performances from my book series "Best Stocks", my own and the guru's.

1   Pointers from short-term gurus

- Develop a trading system that fits your personality, your skill and your timing available for trading. A beginner's trading system is different from a skilled trader's system.
- Start with two or three technical indicators (SMA is my favorite), current events more than fundamentals. Study daily news about the stock you want to trade.
- Even with a win-loss ratio of 50%, you still can make a lot of money by protecting your portfolio with stop loss and your profits with trailing stops. Define and enforce your exit strategy.
- Knowledge is everything, and hence learn from the best traders. There are schools (some on-line) teaching folks how to trade. It is less expensive than paying your tuition via actual trading. This book and most other books are a good start and most cost effective. Many old books (so is this book 15 years later if I do not update it) and old techniques may not work today; today we have no commission brokers, and most technical indicators are available free.

- Beginners cannot beat professionals without luck. You do not gain knowledge by paper trading. Start small. Never risk the money you cannot afford to lose.
- Need basic capital for trading and a laptop to start. Plus living expenses for a few months if you trade full time. Prepare your new venture psychologically. Be emotionally detached in investing. Silence is golden, the rule I just violated. Your friends will not share their wins but blame, and it affects your ego and your trading.
  I know many made so much in 2000 and in early 2021 that they quitted their day jobs, and then they found out they had big losses later.

- Diversify but not over-diversify. Most of us can handle about three trades simultaneously, or more if your holding period is longer than a day.
- When the number of new heights exceeds the new lows by a large margin (determined by you as all markets are different), consider sell (the market could be peaking). Buy, vice versa.
- Day traders may close their positions (more long than short) at the end of the day, especially on late Fridays to avoid unexpected events and interests. The exception is when the market is surging. Learn money management – never bet it all in one trade. Do not trade in the first hour of the market.

- When you have three unsuccessful trades in a row, it is time to take a break and/or switch to paper trading. Better double your bet on winning stocks, and not the other way round.
- Record all your trades and the results in a trade journal. Review it and learn from your successes and losses periodically.
- Modify your trade system according to your gained knowledge and the market trend. Test it out with no or minimum money until you are comfortable.

Links: https://www.youtube.com/watch?v=qL7Z7XQ6tPA

2   Tips from Peter Lynch

He made a lot of money for his investors in Magellan's fund. I came in late to his funds, but I also left early when he retired early in 1990. Many did not want to leave due to the potential tax burdens. His successors never achieved the same performance in Peter's 9 years with the fund. Peter was smart enough to know that his fund was so big that it was the market, and no one could beat the market by that margin consistently.

The following is my summary and my comments on his tips from several YouTube videos
https://www.youtube.com/watch?v=IhnfqbIiGC4
https://www.youtube.com/watch?v=J1DFMXL2kXE
https://www.youtube.com/watch?v=OlYU40sZsUo

1. Study more stocks and pick the best.
   Same as doing your homework.
2. Emotionally detached. Do not sell at the bottom.
   No one can predict the market and is correct constantly. My article could limit the loss and save the cash for reentering the market. Buying at early recovery is very profitable.
3. Investing in companies whose products / services you understand.
   We all have expertise in our own field and the mall is a better place to find good consumer products.
   However, today's mall is pretty much destroyed by Amazon.com. In this case, you should buy Amazon.com, and short many retail outfits and the mall owners. Also check whether Amazon.com has reached its growth potential or not. You may miss Zoom, but as of 10/2020, the stock is too expensive. With the momentum, I do not want to short this stock.
   Made big profits in McDonald's as the sales/profits had been rising for years. However, most of the profits were derived from real estate holdings.
   I do not totally agree with it. There are many companies that we do not know but we can learn and understand what their technologies could be potentially profitable. Buffett did not invest in Apple as he did not use a mobile phone, but his research team should.

4. Easier to beat the professionals than expected.
   Fund managers have to stick with large companies and they cannot time the market. You
5. Invest in profitable small companies.
   Small companies have a lot of risk, but they also have higher profit potential than matured companies.
6. Find a few good stocks particularly at their early stage.
   It is harder to do than say. When the stock moves from Russell 2000 to Russell 1000 (promoting from an index for smaller stocks), they could be candidates. He recommends to keep 5 to 10 stocks for individuals
   A fast growing stock may never be too late to invest.
   We can find these stocks earlier than the professionals and many funds cannot invest in these stocks.
7. Buy growing companies and sell the matured companies that their markets have been saturated (i.e. no place to grow). That's why P/E may not work all the time; you need to consider quarter-to-quarter sales growth and earnings growth; actually year-to-year for the past 5 or even more years is important.
8. Buy good cynical stocks at the bottom and sell at the top.
   It is hard to determine the bottom and the top. However, you need to ensure the company would not go bankrupt by ensuring the income can service its debt.
9. Do not be afraid to buy the stocks that have doubled the prices as long as the fundamentals are still increasing such as Microsoft and Apple.
10. Consider turnaround companies.
    Check the balance sheet. They need cash for turnaround such as promoting new products/services. Skip those companies that have hints of failure of the turnaround. Disney was one at one time by using the hidden assets. Brand names are not included in the financial statements.
11. Do not sell when you double the profit or you lose 10%.
    Agree if they are good stocks. I have some 'good' stocks that went to almost zero value; one Chinese solar company was due to the U.S. policy banning it to the U.S. market.
12. Sell a stock when the fundamentals decline.
    That's where my score for fundamentals or Fidelity's Equity Summary Score comes in. If you do not have time to research stock, buy ETFs that simulate the market. It is not Lynch's idea (as a fund manager) but mine and Buffett's.
13. Do not sell when they have short-term problems such as not meeting the earnings prediction.
14. Do not time the market. I do not agree with this as I have proven simple market timing could save you further losses when the market crashes.
15. In the long term, stocks beat bonds and CDs. Investing in retirement accounts allows our investments to grow, compounding and deferring taxes.

3 Charles Munger: 12 common mistakes

Check out the link https://www.youtube.com/watch?v=W0W44Ykdojw

I add my experiences and also my own common mistakes from mistake #14 and on.

1. Ignore jealousy and resentment.
- I published an article titled "Amazing Returns". I received a lot of resentment and attacks. If they just bought the stocks I recommended, they should have made a lot of money.
- A reader gave me the worst rating on one of my books in the "Best Stock Series" while most ratings were the best. She complained the book was 'too thin'. Most books on investing are 250 pages (6*9), and mine is 300 pages. If she had followed the recommendations of the book, she would have beaten the market by a wide margin.
2. Never open-spend your income. I am guilty of under spending my income.
3. Grab all opportunities.
- I did not invest heavily in Chinese ETFs such as FXI during China's rise, and I did not short them when the U.S. delisted many Chinese stocks.
- I did not take the opportunities when the pandemic was confirmed, but I did invest in commodities due to inflation.
4. Keep learning. I should have read my own book again as I have committed the same investing mistakes.
5. Deserve what you want.
6. Understand your competency. If you do not have time, or desire to learn investing, buy ETFs.
7. Be a survivor. Never put all eggs in one basket (i.e. diversify).
8. Practice the right approach. Check whether your approach is appropriate to the current market conditions from my interpretation.
9. Understand your trade. If it is a value stock, emphasize fundamentals and allow more time for the market to realize its value. Have an exit plan.
10. Invest in trust. He may mean trusting the management of the company.
11. Survive competently as you can.
12. Don't pity yourself. Learn from your failure and ensure that you will not repeat the same mistake. I am guilty as charged.
13. Don't diversify. I interpret "Don't diversify excessively". I believe 5 to 10 stocks with less than 25% of the stocks in the same sector.
14. Don't be afraid of price appreciation as long as the story why you bought the stock has not changed.

4 Making 20% return year after year

This web article (https://www.youtube.com/watch?v=G9xVNjJBSzg) is interesting. Most ideas have been described in this book. I include their pointers here with my own comments:

12. Invest, not speculate. Treat your stock as a company (Buffett's idea). Buy low and sell high. No need to watch your stock every day. Review it periodically by following articles on the stocks you bought via Finviz.com and many other sources.
13. Avoid fees. Broker commissions are free from many sources such as Fidelity. Do not invest via hedge funds. If you do not have time for research, buy an ETF such as SPY.
14. Value investing. You only sell when it has met your investing objective, and/or the fundamentals of the company have changed for the worse. Use Fidelity's Equity Summary Score. Do not buy stocks with a score less than 7 unless you have good reasons.
15. Buy below intrinsic value. Forward Earnings / Price (> 5%) is a good measure with low Debt / Equity (< .5 with some exceptions for industries that require high debts) and no Insider dumping (> -10%). They are all available from Finviz.com.
16. Be patient. Value stocks need time (a year or more) for Wall Street to recognize their values.
    Accumulate cash when the market is risky and expensive. Practice market timing that would tell you to exit the market when the market is plunging.
17. The market is not efficient, and hence blind investing usually leads to losses. It means the market could be overpriced or underpriced. When the P/E of SPY is over 18 (from ETFdb.com), most likely the market is overpriced.
18. Have plenty of cash or liquidity. Hence you are ready when opportunity comes (similar to Rule #5).
19. Average down only if the fundamental metrics agree. I do not average down with some exceptions such as GameStop. Many stocks go bankrupt, averaging down could amplify your loss.
20. Rebalance your portfolio. Do not have more than 30% of your portfolio in one sector. With the exception of sector ETFs, most ETFs have diversified into many stocks with various sectors. I prefer 10 stocks or 5 for a smaller portfolio. Check out the stocks you own periodically (a month or more frequently depending on your time available. Finviz should have many articles on your stocks.
21. Know what you are doing and be consistent. Knowledge is important.
22. I add the following rule: Do not be afraid of high flyers or stocks making new highs. Protect your portfolio with stops.

5 From a guru (technical analysis)

This strategy is from a guru with my modifications.

- Always trade with the trend (buy in upward trend and sell short in downward trend). Again selling short is not for beginners. I use buy for illustration.

  The guru prefers the short-term trend (SMA-20, Simple Moving average from Finviz.com), intermediate-trend (SMA-50) and long-term trend (SMA-200). If the percentages are all positive, it is a buy.

  I prefer the trend for the stock, the sector that the stock belongs to (use the related sector ETF) and the market (use SPY to simulate the market). Hence you have a total of 3 trends. In practice, it is hard to have all 3 trends to be practiced. The trend of the stock is most important, and then followed by the sector.

- Average up (NOT average down). You add your bet on the stock that is moving up. Most traders do not do that, as they think they are paying more than before.

- Use trailing stops to protect your trade on rising stocks and regular stops after you place a buy. Close the position when the stock is too risky, your reasons for the purchase are satisfied, or you have a better stock to buy. When you are not sure, sell half of the position.

- Buy back the stock that you just closed, when the conditions are favorable (trends for example).

- Prepare a trade journey. You want to repeat your success stories and avoid your failures.

6   Predictions for 2021

The following is from a Bloomberg article with my comments. Most will not happen. If it starts to materialize, consult your financial advisor before taking actions accordingly. Again, I am not liable for any actions. This article is written on 12/2020.
https://www.bloomberg.com/news/articles/2020-12-15/if-2020-wasn-t-enough-stanchart-has-eight-big-risks-for-2021

1. We will find out soon whether the U.S. Senate will be dominated by Democrats with the result of Georgia's seats. If the Democrats control the senate, then "Technology shares plummet and U.S. Treasury Yields surge on supply fears".

   My comment: It is easier to pass the proposed laws without fierce opposition. I prefer the opposition party to give reasons for rejecting and/or how to amend any proposed laws instead of just saying "No".

2. "U.S. and China find common ground". Yuan would be appreciated.

   My comment: It would likely happen as Biden is less confrontational than Trump. Yuan's appreciation would cause the U.S. consumers and Chinese exporters. If they take out the bans on Huawei, actually it would be good for the U.S. chip suppliers to China in the long run.

3. "Monetary and fiscal stimulus drives the strongest recovery... Copper rallies 50%".

   My comment: It also adds to our national debt. It would have inflation, lower our competitive edge and shake our USD as the reserve currency. Most investors should have 5 to 20% in gold ETFs and/or gold miners.

4. "Oil prices fall back to $20 barrel".
   My comment. $40 is my estimate if it happens. Many oil companies have good forward P/Es. In some locations, green energy is about the same price as oil. OPEC has not been united.

5. "EUR/USD falls to 1.06 by midyear". No comment as there are too many other factors.

6. "Dollar crashes 15%". It is likely to me. That is why we should use gold and metal as a hedge.

7. "Emerging-market debt defaults... equities fall 30% by second quarter".

   My comment. Likely, as they have been overly extended. China may forget some debts in building their infrastructure. Avoid this risky market as the "potential reward / risk" is not justified.

8. "Biden steps down...Sharp correction in the U.S. equities...dollar decline accelerates".

   My comment: I predicted the same in my article "Disaster in 2020 and 2021". I also predicted the VP will be the first woman president within 5 years for many reasons including Chinese astronomy:

   - Due to bad health; not a surprise for his old age.
   - Unable to unite the divided country.
   - Poor economy leading to high unemployment and poor stock market. '

I also add my own prediction here. China would be the only developed country that has a positive GDP in 2020. The U.K. may have another year of depression due to the new strain of the virus, exit from EU and China's revenge actions similar to Australia.

China recovered from this pandemic in less than 90 days and the factories started to return to normal in April, 2020. The bottleneck now is lack of ships and containers to export their products. If it continues in 2021, China's GDP could be back to 7% (some even predicted 20%). With "One Belt, One Road" and an expanding economy, their digital currency would challenge our mighty USD. Despite the U.S. delisting, I expect Chinese stocks will gain after 2023.

As of 2/2021, our economy is deteriorating fast (judging from the unemployment figure and the no. of bankruptcy), but the market is up due to the excessive printing of money. Our margin debt is at record high. I bet when the market crashes, it will be steep – prepare yourself using stops for example. The pandemic seems to be under control soon. However, I do not bet on hotels and airlines, as most business conferences can be conducted via Zoom. At the same time, I do not want to short Zoom.

Link: One's opinion 2
https://www.youtube.com/watch?v=ZMFTsZraau0&t=661s
https://www.youtube.com/watch?v=D_GmXf7Hk2Y

7   Disrupting innovation

New technologies may change our lives. It would profit our prosperity by investing in the right companies that would profit from these technologies and divesting from the companies that these technologies would harm them. These companies do not usually perform in a down market.

There have been many disruptive technologies in the past. Roughly I divided it into the following phases in our recent history: Phase 1 (electricity and steam engine), Phase 2 (computer), Phase 3 (internet) and today's Phase 4.

Many technologies converge or are implemented in one sector such as 5G and battery technology into self-driving cars. With the exceptions of 5G and Blockchain that are too wide a topic to summarize here, the following will be described briefly and several links are available to further your research. Some are materializing today in 2020 and they should affect us for the coming decade. Most are fundamentally unsound by our metrics.

- Electric cars. Eventually they will outsold combustion cars. Companies: Tesla and battery research companies. Badly affected companies: auto companies that do not adapt and oil companies.
- Energy renewable technology. Eventually, cost per energy unit would favor them compared to oil.
- Robots would affect jobs.
- Fintech. Almost all Chinese consumers are using mobile phones as their wallets and it will not be too long for the U.S. to accept mobile payments. Companies: PayPal and Square. Retails and restaurants could harm their profits in 2021. Badly affected companies: banks that do not adapt.
- Cryptocurrency. Eventually there will be less than 5 and most are issued by banks and countries with good records.
- Gene modifying companies. It has fixed many and continues to fix many diseases by reprograming bad genes. Companies: CRIPR. Badly affected companies: drug companies that do not cooperate with CRISPR, Editas Medicine and Intellia Therapeutics.
- AI, artificial intelligence. We have good research but our privacy restriction limits our implementation.
- As of today 3/2021, most of these companies have suffered big losses recently. We should use trailing stops (such as 5 to 10%) to protect our investments. Most of these companies do not have earnings. It is like building castles in the sky. Many of these stocks are rotated to travel stocks due to the effective vaccines.

Links: Cathy Wood 1 2 3. As of 1/2021, it is too risky and signs of peaking appear.
https://www.youtube.com/watch?v=eE6u67Ph768
https://www.youtube.com/watch?v=hLnOoXopfow
https://www.youtube.com/watch?v=LS7lVaW8mvY

Epilogue

I do not believe that this book or any book can be the Holy Grail of investing. However, it has a lot of fresh ideas and good pointers that have brought me financial success (at least so far). I ask my readers to challenge my pointers and ensure they are applicable in today's market and meet their own objectives and requirements.

A good pointer can make you thousands of dollars, and a bad or misinterpreted one can do the opposite. Always do paper trading on any strategy and / or idea before you commit real money to it. Start your strategy with cash in small increments until you have more confidence.

Use the links in this book for reference and understand how we come to the conclusions. This book and similar books provide you ways on how to make decisions based on current events that can be obtained from TV, the internet and magazines.

Hopefully, this book's primary objective of enabling you to be a better investor is met.

I will practice what I preach and what I've learned from writing this book. Jesse Livermore was probably one of our greatest traders ever. Yet he ended up losing most of his money and then killed himself. The major reason was he did not follow what he preached. We need to diversify our investments and it is better to be a turtle investor. Recently a 20-year-old, Robinhood trader killed himself after losing $730,000.

A link is provided for future updates and announcements.
https://ebmyth.blogspot.com/2020/01/updates.html
My blog:
https://tonyp4idea.blogspot.com/

Final notes

Thanks for reading this book and I hope it will be beneficial to your financial health. If so, comment on it on Amazon.com or the place you bought this book. I will be very grateful.

My parting gifts to you

The printed book costs too much to include non-essential articles, and you do not want to cut down trees. Some articles may be included in this book already.

- Investment advices
  https://ebmyth.blogspot.com/2020/01/book-14-investment-advices.html
- On economy
  https://ebmyth.blogspot.com/2020/03/the-economy.html
- More on investment strategies
  https://ebmyth.blogspot.com/2020/03/investing-strategies.html
- More on China
  https://ebmyth.blogspot.com/2020/09/on-china.html
- More on bonuses current events
  https://ebmyth.blogspot.com/2020/03/bonuses.html
- Update of my books. Best Stocks to buy for 2020. Available in 12/15/2020. Not a promise.
  https://ebmyth.blogspot.com/2020/01/updates.html

#Filler "How to make a 50% return"
https://www.youtube.com/watch?v=eEto5nEkf1Y
#Filler Buffett, the person.
https://www.youtube.com/watch?v=w-eX4sZi-Zs
#Filler: People with power + People with money = Corruption

Appendix 1 – All my books

- Complete the Art of Investing (highly recommended combining most of my books on investing). The Kindle version has over 850 pages (6*9), about 3 times the size of an investing book.
- Sector Rotation: 21 Strategies and another book Shorting (highly recommended for short-term investors) have more specific chapters on the topic and share many articles with "Complete the art of investing".
- Best stocks for 2022 (avail after Dec. 15, 2021).
- "Nuclear War with China".
- Books for today's market: Profit from Coming Market Crash.

- The following books are in a series: Finding Profitable Stocks, Market Timing and Scoring Stocks. Alternate books: Using Fidelity and Using Finviz.
- Books on strategies: "Profit from bull, bear and sideways markets" (Rotation + Momentum + ETF Rotation + trend following), Trading System (similar to printed version of Complete), Swing (Rotation + Momentum), ETF Rotation for Couch Potatoes, Momentum, SuperStocks, Dividend, Penny & Micro Stock, and Retiree.
- Books for advance beginners: Be an expert (highly recommended), Introduce, Investing for Beginners, Beat Fund Managers, Profit via ETFs, Buffett, Ideas, Conservative and Top-Down.
- Miscellaneous: Lessons in Investing. Investing Strategies. Buy Low and Sell High. Buy High and sell Higher. Buffettology. Technical Analysis. Trading Stocks.
- Concise Editions and Introduction Editions are available at very low prices and are competitive with books of similar sizes (50 pages) and prices ($3 range).

Most books have paperbacks. Links and offers are subject to change without notice.

Best stocks to buy for 2022 (avail. after Dec. 15, 21)

We care about performance only. Not considering dividends and fees, my last three books in this series have beaten the SPY (the market to most) by **110%, 71% and 25%** from the publish date to 07/01/2021.

Book	Stocks	Return	Ann.	Beat SPY by
Best Book for 2021 2nd Edition	10	20%	52%	110%
Best Book for 2021	4	29%	52%	71%
Best Book to Buy from Aug, 2020	14	42%	45%	25%
Avg.	9	31%	50%	69%

Appendix 2 – Complete the Art of Investing

Instead of buying 16 books, why not buy one book (Complete the Art of Investing) consisting of 16 books? Besides saving money and your digital shelve space, it gives you quick reference and concentration on the topic you're currently interested in. It covers most investing topics in investing excluding speculative investing such as currency trading and day trading. The Kindle version has about 850 pages (6*9), about the size of three books of average size. With the cost of $10 and at least 850 investing ideas, it is about one cent per idea. Most other books have only a few ideas in the entire book

The 16 books
This book "Complete Art of Investing" is divided into 16 books as follows. Click for the link to the book described in Amazon.com. I squeezed more than 3,000 pages into 850 pages by eliminating duplicated information such as evaluating stocks.

Book No.	Amazon.com
1	Simple techniques
2	Finding Stocks
3	Evaluating Stocks
4	Scoring Stocks
5	Trading Stocks
6	Market Timing
7	Strategies
8	Sector Rotation
9	Insider Trading
10	Penny Stocks & Micro Cap
11	Momentum Investing
12	Dividend Investing
13	Technical Analysis
14	Investing Ideas
15	The Economy
16	Buffettology

The book links are subject to change without notice.

"How to be a billionaire" is for beginners and couch potatoes, who can use the advanced features of this book in the simplest and less time-consuming techniques. Most advance users can skip this section unless they want to use some of the short cuts described.

We start with the basic books Finding Stocks, Evaluate Stocks, Trading Stocks and Market Timing. You can select and start with one of the many styles and strategies in investing such as swing trading and top-down strategy. Many tools are described in other books such as ETFs, technical analysis, covered calls and trading plan.

Many books start with "Why" to lure you to read more and are followed by "How" and then the theory behind the book.
If the book you're reading is beneficial to you, imagine how it would with 850 pages.

\# Most readers' comments are on "Debunk the Myths in Investing", which this book is originally based on. As of 2018, I did not know any of the commentators on my books.

"I skipped ahead to his chapter book 14 (of "Complete the Art of Investing"), Investment Advice just to get a feel of his writing style. His research is phenomenal and doesn't overwhelm with big words or catchy "sales-like" tactics.

I truly believe this ordinary man, Mr. Tony Pow, has a gift of explaining his experience as an investor without the bull crap of trying to make you buy his stuff. He seemingly just wants to share his knowledge, tips, and clarity of definitions for the kind of folks like me who want to understand something FIRST before jumping in with emotions of trying to make a boat load of money. I like the technical analysis side he brings.

Mr. Tony Pow talks about hidden gems in his book; well....quite frankly, he is a hidden gem. Thank you and I will also post my comments about this author to my Facebook page!" – JB on this book.

"Excellent book, recommend to all investors... great knowledge. It has fine-tuned my investing strategies... Your book is hard to set aside, as I read it all the time learning good techniques and analysis of stocks, ETF... Since I purchased your book in March, I have underlined, highlighted and placed tabs on top of pages for quick reference." – Aileron on this book.

"Tony, I just finished reading your 2nd edition. It's my pleasure to report that I found it most interesting. You're welcome to use this blurb if you like:

Debunk the Myths in Investing is an all-encompassing look at not only the most salient factors influencing markets and investors, but also a from-the-trenches look at many of the misconceptions and mistakes too many investors make. Reading this book may save not only time and aggravation but money as well!"

Joseph Shaefer, CEO, Stanford Wealth Management LLC.

"Tony, Great work!" from James and Chris, who are portfolio managers.

"'Debunk the Myths in Investing' is a comprehensive book on investing that deals with many aspects of this tense profession in which with a lot of knowledge and a bit of luck (or vice versa) one can greatly benefit...

Therefore 'Debunk the Myths in Investing' is an interesting book that on its 500 pages offer a lot of knowledge related to investing world and many practical advice, so I can recommend its reading if you're interested in this topic."
- Denis Vukosav, Top 500 Reviewers at Amazon.com.

"490 pages (Debunk) of a genius's ranting and hypothesis with various theories throughout, written light-heartedly with ample doses of humor...Yes, the myth of not being able to profitably time the market is BUSTED...

One might ask... Why is he giving away the results of his hard-earned research for only $20? He states that his children are not interested in investing and wants to share his efforts with the world." - Abe Agoda.

"Excellent book, recommend to all investors... great knowledge. It has fine-tuned my investing strategies... Your book is hard to set aside, as I read it all the time learning good techniques and analysis of stocks, ETF... Since I purchased your book in March, I have underlined, highlighted and placed tabs on top of pages for quick reference." - Aileron on this book.

"Great stuff, Tony. It's great to meet experienced traders such as yourself. I had a browse through the book and think your method is a little more refined than mine."
"Your strategy is very rules based and solid. I sometimes envy people who have developed something like this."

Making 50% in one month
I claim to have the best one-month performance ever for recommending 8 or more stocks without using options and leverage. My following return is

57% in a month or 621% annualized. They are slightly different as I calculated the average from the averages of three different accounts. The average buy date is 12/26/18 and the "current date" is 01/28/19.

The performance may not be repeated. I will use the same screen for the coming years and even the expected 10% (or 120% annualized) is very good.

I used the same screen for searching stock candidates. I spent a total of about 20 hours from Dec. 15, 2018 to Jan. 5, 2019.

Stock	Buy Price	Sold or Current Price	Buy date	Sold or Current date	Profit %	Profit % Ann.	Status
CHK	2.13	2.99	01/03/09	01/18/19	40%	982%	Sold
MNK	16.41	21.45	01/03/19	01/25/19	31%	510%	Sold
MNK	16.43	21.45	01/03/19	01/25/19	31%	507%	Sold
NNBR	5.68	8.58	12/26/18	01/28/19	51%	565%	
NNBR	5.72	8.58	12/26/18	01/28/19	66%	727%	
ESTE	4.35	6.45	12/26/18	01/18/19	48%	766%	Sold
LCI	4.61	8.29	12/21/18	01/28/19	80%	767%	
MDR	8.01	9.13	01/08/19	01/28/19	14%	255%	
YRCW	3.29	5.78	12/21/18	01/28/19	76%	727%	
YRCW	3.26	5.78	12/21/18	01/28/19	77%	742%	
ASRT	3.56	4.18	12/26/18	01/28/19	17%	193%	
UTCC	7.13	11.00	12/26/18	01/28/19	54%	600%	
YRCW	2.92	5.78	12/26/18	01/28/19	98%	1083%	

Best one-year return

I claim to have the best-performed article in Seeking Alpha history, an investing site, for recommending 15 or more stocks in one year after the publish date without using options and leverage.

https://seekingalpha.com/article/1095671-amazing-returns-velti-alcatel-lucent-alpha-natural-resources

Your choice

"Complete the art of investing" should be your first choice. If you are short-term trading, I recommend "Sector Rotation: 21 Strategies" and "Shorting Stocks /ETFs". These 3 books together with "Using Fidelity" share many articles.

My recommended stocks can be found in my "Best stocks" series. It would be published on Dec. 15 – it is not a promise. So far, this book and "Sector Rotation: 21 Strategies" are my best sellers. All info are subject to change without notice.

Sector Rotation: 21 Strategies

In addition, as of 5/2020 I bet that no author besides me made **over 4 times** using sector rotation starting the amount more than his yearly salary then.

- On 5/26/2020, I searched for "Sector Rotation" under Amazon's Book. They are listed in the same order except my book Sector Rotation: 21 Strategies.

Book	Date	Size[1]	Kindle $[1]	Hard $
Sector Rotation: 21 Strategies	**05/2020**	**425**	**$9.95**	$24.95
Super Sectors	09/2010	289	$26.39	$49.95
Dual Momentum Investing	11/2014	240	$40.40	$42.20
Sector Investing	05/1996	260		$29.94
Sector Trading Strategies	08/2007	164	$26.39	$16.66
The Sector Strategist	03/2012	225	$26.39	$44.96
ETF Rotation	10/2012	125	**$9.95**	**$14.99**
Optimal... Sector Rotation	07/2015	80		$44.07

[1] From Amazon on size and prices as of 5/25/2020. Last update is 09/2021.

My book won in all categories except the price for hard copy in one. However, my book won as the lowest cost per page by a wide margin.

- I have **21** strategies in sector rotation while most books have only one. It ranges from simple rotation of a stock ETF and cash for beginners to many advanced strategies for experts. Most other books have one or two strategies.
- Andrew, a contributor on Sector Rotation article at Seeking Alpha, said, "Great stuff, Tony. It's great to meet experienced traders such as yourself. I had a browse through the book and think your method is a little more refined than mine."
- "You have written the book in a way that makes good and logical sense." Bill.
- Do not be fooled by past performances. Just check the recent performance of the top 50 stocks selected by IBD in the last five years. The mediocre result (hopefully it will change) could be due to too many followers and/or there is no evergreen strategy.
- I switched most (if not all) of my sector funds in April, 2000 from technology sectors to traditional sectors (better to money market fund). We can reduce losses by spotting market plunges and the sector trend.

Appendix 3 - Our window to the investing world

The paperback version of this chapter can be found in the following link.
http://ebmyth.blogspot.com/2013/11/web-sites.html

- **General**
  Wikipedia / Investopedia /Yahoo!Finance / MarketWatch / Cnnfn / Morningstar /CNBC / Bloomberg / WSJ / Barron's / Motley Fool / TheStreet

- **Evaluate stocks**
  Finviz / SeekingAlpha / MSN Money / Zacks / Daily Finance / ADR / Fidelity / Earnings Impact / OpenInsider / NYSE / NASDAQ / SEC / SEC for 10K and 10Q (quarterly) reports required to file for listed stocks in major exchanges.

- **Charts**
  BigCharts / FreeStockCharts / StockCharts /

- **Screens**
  Yahoo!Finance / Finviz / CNBC / Morningstar /

- **Besides stocks**
  123Jump / Hoover's Online / FINRA Bond Market Data / REIT / Commodity Futures / Option Industry

- **Vendors**
  AAII / Zacks / IBD / GuruFocus / VectorVest / Fidelity / Interactive Brokers / Merrill Lynch /

- **Economy.**
  Econday / EcoconStats / Federal Reserve / Economist /

- **Misc.**
  Dow Jones Indices / Russell / Wilshire / IRS / Wikinvest / ETF Database / ETF Trends / Nolo (estate planning) / AARP /

Appendix 4 - ETFs / Mutual Funds

What is an ETF

ETFs have basic differences from mutual funds: 1. Lower management expenses, 2. Trade ETFs same as stocks, and 3. Usually more diversified but not more selective than the related mutual funds such as NOBL vs FRDPX.

The major classifications of ETFs are 1. Simulating an index such as SPY, QQQ and DIA, 2. Simulating a sector such as XLE and SOXX, 3. Simulating an asset class such as GLD and SLV, 4. Simulating a country or a group of countries such as EWC and FXI, 5. Managed by a manager(s) such as ARKK, 6. Betting a market or sector to go down such as SH and PSQ, and 7. Leveraged (not recommended for beginners).

Fidelity: Index ETFs (https://www.fidelity.com/etfs/overview).

Wikipedia on ETF (http://en.wikipedia.org/wiki/Exchange-traded_fund).

List of ETFs
ETF database (Recommended): http://etfdb.com/
ETF Bloomberg: http://www.bloomberg.com/markets/etfs/
ETF Trends: http://www.etftrends.com/
A list of ETFs. Seeking Alpha.
http://etf.stock-encyclopedia.com/category/)
A list of contra ETFs (or bear ETFs)
http://www.tradermike.net/inverse-short-etfs-bearish-etf-funds/
Misc.: ETFGuide, ETFReplay
Fidelity low-cost index funds:
https://www.youtube.com/watch?v=zpKi4_IJvIY
Fidelity Annuity funds with performance data.
http://fundresearch.fidelity.com/annuities/category-performance-annual-total-returns-quarterly/FPRAI?refann=005

Other resources
Most subscription services offer research on ETFs. IBD has a strategy dedicated to ETFs and so does AAII to name a couple.

Seeking Alpha has extensive resources for ETF including an ETF screener and investing ideas. So is ETFdb.

Not all ETFs are created equal

Check their performances and their expenses.

When to use or not to use ETFs

I prefer sector mutual funds in some industries, as they have many bad stocks such as drug industry, banks, miners and insurers. Most mutual funds cannot time the market.

When you believe a sector is heading up (or contra ETF for heading down), but you do not have time to do research on specific stocks, buy an ETF for the sector; it is same for the market.

Half ETF

Taking out half of the stocks that score below the average in an index ETF could beat the same full ETF itself. I call it HETF (half the ETF). You heard it here first. To illustrate, sort the expected P/E (not including stocks with negative earnings) in ascending order and only include the stocks on the first half. Add more fundamental metrics. It will take a few minutes.

Disadvantages of ETFs

- When you have two stocks in a sector ETF one good one and one bad one, the ETF treats them the same. Stock pickers would buy the one that has a better appreciation potential.
- Sometimes the return could be misleading due to stock rotation. To illustrate this, on August 29, 2012, SHLD was replaced by LYB in a sector fund. SHLD was down by 4% and LYB was up by 4% primarily due to the switch. Unless you sell and buy at the right time (which is impossible), your return would not match the ETF's returns due to the replacement.
- Ensure the performance matches the corresponding index; it is hard due to excluding dividends.

Advantages of ETFs

- We have demonstrated that you can beat the market by using market timing. Between 2000 and Nov., 2013, you only exit and reenter the market 3 times and the result is astonishing.
- It is easy to rotate a sector vs. buying/selling all of the stocks in this sector. Rotating a sector is the same as trading a stock.
- The risk is spread out, and your portfolio is diversified especially for a market ETF or buying three or more ETFs in different sectors.
- Periodically the bad stocks in most funds are replaced by better stocks.
- Eliminate the time in researching stocks.

Leveraged ETFs

I do not recommend them. Some are 2x, 3x and even higher. They're too risky for beginners. However, when you are very sure or your tested strategy has very low drawdown, you may want to use them to improve performance. Most leveraged ETFs and contra ETFs have higher fees.

My basic ETF tables

I include some contra ETFs, mutual funds and Fidelity's annuity. Some of these may be interesting to you.

ETFs and funds come and go. Some ideas and classifications are my own interpretation. Refer to ETFdb for updated information. Not responsible for any error. Check out the ETF or fund before you take any action.

Table by market cap:

Category	ETF	Mutual Funds	Fidelity's Annuity	Contra ETF	Alternate
Size:					
Large Cap	DIA	See Blend		DOG	
	SPY			SH	FXAIX
					VOO
	QQQ			PSQ	FNCMX
	RYH				
Blend	IWD	BEQGX			
Growth	SPYG	FBGRX			FSPGX
Value	SPYV	DOGGX			FLCOX
Dividend	NOBL	FRDPX			
	VYM				
Mid Cap			FNBSC	MYY	
Blend	MDY	VSEQX			
Growth		STDIX			
		BPTRX			
Value		FSMVX			
Small Cap			FPRGC	SBB	FSSNX
Blend	IWM	HDPSX			
Growth		PRDSX			FECGX
Value		SKSEX			FISVX
Micro	IWC				
Multi					
Blend		VDEOX			
Growth		VHCOX			

Value		TCLCX				
Total						FSKAX
Bond						
Long Term (20)	VLV	BTTTX		TBF		
Mid Term (7 – 10)	VCIT	FSTGX				
Short Term (1 – 3 yrs.)	VCSH	THOPX				
Total	BOND	PONDX				
Corp Invest Grade	VCIT	NTHEX				
High Yield (junk)	PHB	SPHIX				
Muni	MUB	Check state				
Special situation						
Buy back	PKW					

Table by sectors:

Sector	ETF	Mutual Funds	Fidelity's Annuity
Banking[1]		FSRBK	
Regional	IAT		
Bio Tech	IBB	FBIOX	
	XBI	Large	
Consumer Dis.	XLY	FSCPX	FVHAC
Consumer Staple	XLP	FDFAX	FCSAC
Finance	KIE	FIDSX	FONNC
	IYF		
Energy	XLE	FSENX	FJLLC
Energy Service		FSESX	
Gold	GLD	FSAGX	
Gold Miner	GDX	VGPMX	
Health Care	IYH	FSPHX	FPDRC
	VHT	VGHCX	
House Builder	ITB	FSHOX	
	ITB	Perform	
Industrial	IYJ	FCYIX	FBALC
Material	VAW	FSDPX	

		IYM		
Oil		USO		
Oil Service		OIH	FSESX	
Oil Exploration		XOP		
Real Estate		VNQ	FRIFX	FFWLC
REIT		VNQ		
Retail		RTH	FSRPX	
		XRT		
Regional bank		KRE	FSRBX	
Semi Conduct		SMH		
Software		XSW	FSCSX	
		IGV		
Technology		XLK	FSPTX	FYENC
		FDN	FBSOX	
			ROGSX	
Telecomm.		VOX	FSTCX	FVTAC
Transport		XTN		
		IYT		
Utilities		XLU	FSUTX	FKMSC
Wireless			FWRLX	

Footnote. [1] Also check Finance.

Table by countries outside the USA:

Country	ETF	Mutual Funds	Fidelity's Annuity	Alternate
Australia	EWA			
Brazil	EWZ			
Canada	EWC	FICDX		
China	FXI	FHKCX		
EAFE	EFA			
Emerging	VWO	FEMEX	FEMAC	FPADX
Europe	VGK	FIEUX		
Global	KXI	PGVFX		
Greece	GREK			
India	INDY	MINDX		
Indonesia	EIDO			
Latin America	ILF	FLATX		
Nordic		FNORX		
Hong Kong	EWH			
Japan	EWJ	FJPNX		
S. Africa	EZA			
S. Korea	EWY	MAKOX		
Singapore	EWS			
Taiwan	EWT			
	TUR			
United Kingdom	EWU			
Foreign:				
Combination				
Intern. Div.	IDV			FTIHX
Small Cap	SCZ			
Value	EFV			
Europe	VGK			

#Filler: Honey, my book can play music.

https://www.youtube.com/watch?v=HxGT5z6d-GA&list=PLMZa6mP7jZ2b1otqG4tfbgZpLEdh6YiNF

It may cut down commercials by casting it to TV.

www.ingramcontent.com/pod-product-compliance
Lightning Source LLC
Chambersburg PA
CBHW060830220526
45466CB00003B/1043